The
Persuasive Actor

Rhetorical Power on the
Contemporary Stage

The
Persuasive Actor

Rhetorical Power on the Contemporary Stage

Milan Dragicevich

an imprint of
Hackett Publishing Company, Inc.
Indianapolis/Cambridge

A Focus book

Focus an imprint of
Hackett Publishing Company

Copyright © 2019 by Hackett Publishing Company, Inc.

All rights reserved
Printed in the United States of America

22 21 20 19   1 2 3 4 5 6 7

For further information, please address
　Hackett Publishing Company, Inc.
　P.O. Box 44937
　Indianapolis, Indiana 46244-0937

　www.hackettpublishing.com

Cover design by Brian Rak
Composition by Integrated Composition Systems

Cataloging-in-Publication data can be accessed via the Library of Congress Online Catalog.

ISBN-13: 978-1-58510-924-1

The paper used in this publication meets the minimum requirements of American National Standard for Information Sciences—Permanence of Paper for Printed Library Materials, ANSI Z39.48–1984.

∞

Contents

Preface   ix

Introduction   xi

Chapter 1 STRETCHING THE TEXT: Balance   1

Chapter 2 POWERING THE TEXT: Amplification   27

Chapter 3 SPEAKING IN CLOSE-UPS: Image & Description   60

Chapter 4 MAKING CONNECTIONS: Metaphor   94

Chapter 5 MANTRAS, SPELLS, and GROOVES: Repetition   124

Chapter 6 TRUSTING THE LANGUAGE   157

Glossary   167

Suggestions for Further Reading   170

Credits and Acknowledgments   171

Index   174

*For Bojana and our boys:
Nikola, Deyan, and Sasha*

speak your dream

PREFACE

This "rhetorical" work began in simple exploratory workshops I organized during my days as an apprentice actor with the Oregon Shakespeare Festival in Ashland. I had a few ideas, lots of passion (and questions), but no roadmap. Certainly no "methodology." That would start to develop years later in Los Angeles, with incremental steps, at the Will Geer Theatricum, where I served as company member and Academy instructor. Those Academy classes provided a kind of open lab, allowing me space to experiment and work with willing actors eager to explore this language-driven performance work. Little by little the work started to reveal itself and I followed its arc as a visiting professor at UCLA, then during my own independent L.A. workshops, and finally to an extended opportunity at the University of Massachusetts Amherst, where I have really expanded, strengthened, and sharpened the verbal training.

First and foremost, I am indebted to Professor Richard Lanham, who, during my undergraduate days at UCLA, opened the door to the rhetorical universe and taught me how to discover the verbal surface. That was the beginning of a fascinating journey. I am thankful to Ellen Geer, Artistic Director of the Will Geer Theatricum, who gave me the freedom, support, and space to develop this work. The Will Geer introduced me to actor-educator Susan Angelo, whose active encouragement and advocacy inspired me to continue the journey. I'm also grateful to the many actors and theater makers who have taken part in the workshops, labs, and classes over the past two decades. They have made this work palpable, infusing it with their voices, skill, and dedicated spirit. It's in the trenches of live performance where this work is tested and where it ultimately comes alive. A special shout-out to my UMass students in our Detonated Language performance classes: your adventurous embrace of the material helped this work grow and take shape.

This book has benefited from insightful suggestions provided by professors Arthur Kinney and Harley Erdman of the University of Massachusetts, as well as Leslie Reidel of the University of Delaware. UMass Professor Melissa Mueller was very helpful in explaining ancient Greek terms for Aristotle's

PREFACE

descriptions of Metaphor. Finally, I want to acknowledge the careful guidance of my editor at Hackett, Brian Rak, whose exacting eye helped clarify and chisel the various arguments and approaches articulated in the following pages.

Milan Dragicevich
University of Massachusetts

INTRODUCTION

Let's go on an adventure. Into a magical land of words. It's a place that celebrates the persuasive power of the spoken word. A place where the intrepid traveler notices how sound and rhythm inform a piece of vibrant communication, the ways language weaves a spell upon the visitor, and how listening is shaped by passionate speaking. To begin this adventure, you will need some essential equipment: your full voice, a dose of courage, a robust imagination, and a hunger to communicate—to move your listener out of apathy and into active engagement.

One more thing. You'll need keen powers of observation. For in this largely unexplored verbal terrain there are exquisite treasures to be found. But interestingly these treasures are not buried deep into the ground but they are scattered all across the surface, waiting for discerning eyes to spot them.

Before we take this journey, we might briefly take note of our point of departure, our current location and coordinates. It will provide context for our travels.

Our confessional early 21st century has favored the expression of spontaneous emotion over the appeal of calculated verbal artifice. We worship feelings, not words. Feelings are sincere; words are sly and treacherous. The more ornamental or heightened the words, the more we stand at arm's length from them, in skeptical discomfort. The Serpent, as we recall, whispered beguiling words to Eve in the Garden and humankind has yet to recover. In our schools, the study of speech (and really, language) is viewed as a painful duty, something akin to watching paint dry. In the classroom, students are no longer required to "stand and deliver." The voice is never unleashed, and the student's very Self remains trapped within.

American actor training, excepting Shakespearean performance, has mirrored this distrust of crafted language over the last century. There exists an unexamined assumption that heightened language belongs to the Shakespearean World, where blank verse and lofty Elizabethan verbiage require careful analysis, while contemporary works are somehow exempt from equally vigorous verbal investigation. Many contemporary plays unwittingly

INTRODUCTION

aid and abet this view, as characters struggle to express deep or hidden emotions, feelings, psychological undercurrents—*behavior beyond words*. The words themselves, the verbal *surface*, are less appealing than what lies beneath the surface—the *subtext*. Actor training today worships subtext, where the words serve primarily as masks for a concealed truth or motive. "It's not about the words" is a mantra one hears in certain contemporary actor training labs.

Subtext is indeed a valuable tool for character analysis and for understanding the emotional undertow of a scene. This is particularly true for those plays featuring "invisible" dialogue, where the words, bereft of their own power, are struggling to express some hidden feelings. Here is an example from a compelling contemporary short play called *Lift and Bang* by Julie Marie Myatt. In the summer heat, a young man, Ben, has come round to visit his former girlfriend, Grace, who is spreading flour on a large wooden table on her back porch.

BEN: I thought it was you out here.
GRACE: Did you. (*Kneading*)
BEN: Looks like you're working hard.
GRACE: Yeah.
BEN: You're always work—
GRACE: Smells like you just got out of the shower.
BEN: My second one today. Goddamn heat.
(*Silence.*)
BEN: Looks like you could do with one.
(*Grace continues kneading.*)
BEN: What are you making?
GRACE: What's it look like?
BEN: Work.
GRACE: Yeah.
BEN: Why are you out here?
GRACE: Kitchen's too hot. Air conditioning's broke.
BEN: You got someone to fix it?
GRACE: Yeah.
BEN: Soon?
GRACE: Yeah.

INTRODUCTION

BEN: What kind is it?
GRACE: Kind's what?
BEN: That bread.
GRACE: Rye.
BEN: Oh. I always liked that kind.
GRACE: How's Beth?

Do you recognize this type of exchange? It has all the strong attributes of subtext-based dialogue. Powerful unreleased emotions are lurking *beneath* the ordinary words. Our attention is diverted not so much to the words themselves as to the pool of feelings gathering *under* the words. The characters are groping for meaning; their words conceal an inner state. Ben cannot find the bravery or honesty to say, "Do you miss me?" or "Do you still have feelings for me?" So he punctuates his conversation with inane statements about Grace's bread making and about fixing the air conditioner.

Grace, on the other hand, cannot express, "Why have you come back here to break my heart again?" So she responds with monosyllables and clipped, broken phrases. Her "yeah" and "What's it looks like?" barely hold back the torrent that's swirling under her words. She finally comes to the knifepoint of her subject with "How's Beth?" The scene suddenly jolts onto another track, one that puts the two characters on a collision course.

This kind of *behavioral* dialogue asks the actor—and the audience—to look beyond the words, to the feelings embedded beneath or in between the words. Pauses, lack of direct communication, words emptied of their own power—these qualities serve to make the language "invisible." Actors are trained to place primary attention on the subtext and to pursue an action. Contemporary actor training relies heavily on this working model. For this kind of play and text, this is a necessary and important methodology.

But let's take a look at another piece of theatrical text, one that may require a very different response to language. In Tom Stoppard's dazzling memory play, *Travesties*, Henry Carr recalls his meeting with the novelist, James Joyce, in Zurich during World War I, where Joyce offers him a leading role in his amateur production of Oscar Wilde's *The Importance of Being Earnest*.

JOYCE: We are short of a good actor to play the lead—he's an articulate and witty English gentleman—

INTRODUCTION

> CARR: Ernest?
> JOYCE: Not Ernest—the other one.
> CARR (*Tempted*): No—no—I absolutely—
> JOYCE: Aristocratic—romantic—epigrammatic—he's a young swell.
> CARR: A swell...?
> JOYCE: He says things like, I may occasionally be a little over-dressed but I make up for it by being immensely over-educated. That gives you the general idea of him.
> CARR: How many changes of costume?
> JOYCE: Two complete outfits.
> CARR: Town or country?
> JOYCE: First one then the other.
> CARR: Indoors or out?
> JOYCE: Both.
> CARR: Summer or winter?
> JOYCE: Summer but not too hot.
> CARR: Not raining?
> JOYCE: Not a cloud in the sky.
> CARR: But he could be wearing—a boater?
> JOYCE: It is expressly stipulated.
> CARR: And he's not—in pyjamas?
> JOYCE: Expressly proscribed.
>
> (Act 1)

This exchange invites us to partake of the pleasures of word play! Our attention is riveted, first and foremost, by the words themselves. Consider the sound play: "aristocra*tic*, roman*tic*, epigramma*tic*." These speakers carefully dish out their words, like pieces of rich dessert: "He's a young *swell*." And notice the ping-pong rhythmic exchanges: "Town or country?/First one then the other./Indoors or out?/Both./Summer or winter?/Summer but not too hot." Little morsels of repetition are also featured, backed by lofty legal rhetoric: "expressly stipulated...expressly proscribed." And Joyce cites an all-time witty zinger from Wilde's play: "I may occasionally be a little over-dressed but I make up for it by being immensely over-educated."

INTRODUCTION

Travesties is a play that begs the actor to *notice the language and play the words*. In a very different—though no less vigorous—way, so does *The Evidence of Silence Broken: A Spoken-Word Performance Concert*, by Zell Miller III. Capturing the birth of a poet's voice (and evolving sense of personal identity), this innovative piece is verbally courageous and unabashed. Here, accompanied by Hip-Hop beats, the Poet, as a kind of MC, takes you into his neighborhood.

> Down 11th Street / walking with skipped strokes / and tuition-free knowledge / gliding with intellect / bending corners in this urban-renewal-gone-bad / …badges and bunches hunch together / can't tell the good from the bad / everybody is looking to get by / get that thing to get you high / induced at seven months there are children here / children here who look like me / I'm a product of these streets /

The first thing you may notice, on the page, are the punctuating slash marks, much like measures in musical notation, giving the language a propulsive rhythm, phrasing, and drive. It's a *charging* speech. The words themselves beckon to you. The poet invites the listener to decode the hip vernacular of his world: "tuition-free knowledge" could be street smarts; or "urban-renewal-gone-bad" might otherwise be called The Projects. But "urban-renewal-gone-bad" has an attitude, a voice. So does "badges and bunches hunch together," where cops ("badges") and gang members ("bunches") coexist, backed by "b" alliteration. Listen to the rhythmic exchanges, too: "gliding with intellect" seems to call back to "walking with skipped strokes." Above all, this entire passage, with its slashes, rhythmic drive, and poetic lingo, invites the audience to *notice the words*.

How does the actor get the audience to notice the words? By paying close attention to the words himself rather than plummeting straight to the depths of subtext. Especially when the words themselves are calling to you. The treasures of language glitter on the *surface* of the text. This approach requires a different mindset, a new awareness that character can be shaped by language, sound and rhythm, and word choice. By scanning the verbal surface or "visible" dialogue, one suddenly discovers clues to the world of the play,

INTRODUCTION

and a panorama of insights into the character's personality, influences, and desires.

In *Travesties* and *The Evidence of Silence Broken*, words matter. Words inform the story. Perhaps no contemporary playwright celebrates language more than Tom Stoppard, whose plays consistently exhibit an astonishing verbal ingenuity. And he has many compatriots across the broad expanse of time. Examine the high-voltage verbal blasts favored by Shakespeare's heroes. Savor the exquisite witty dialogue of 17th-century Restoration theater. Closer to our own time, take a ringside seat at the verbal slugfests that Bernard Shaw unleashed in his plays. Closer still, absorb the gritty poetic pleas in the plays of Suzan-Lori Parks. Listen to the rich sonic landscapes of Tony Kushner's yearning characters or the haunted imagery of August Wilson's world. Hear the slash-and-burn verbal attack of Sarah Kane or Mac Wellman's fractured characters. Buckle up for Hip-Hop theater, where the poets conjure sizzling wordplay, incendiary rhythms, and booming sounds, as they crave sharp, cutting-edge verbal expression. All of these plays and writers vary in their specific styles, but they are united in their quest to harness verbal power. They share a voracious appetite for vibrant words and imaginative language.

These "language" plays require actors who have verbal "chops," as jazz musicians used to say. Verbal training is required. Like a skilled musician, the actor must learn to read the notes and play the riffs and scales. How does the contemporary actor acquire this verbal training today? How does she build verbal awareness and strength, especially in an overly "psychological" climate where words are often devalued?

First we must uncover some forgotten wisdom from long ago by taking a journey across the rich fields of *Surface Text*. We take this journey not to bask in sweet nostalgia for yesterday but to open our eyes to a sparkling vision—which holds exciting knowledge that we can then adapt to our bustling contemporary times even as we reach for the future.

Two thousand five hundred years ago, a new kind of knowledge was being discovered and shaped. For the first time in the history of the West, clustering around the Greek cities of Athens and Syracuse, people began analyzing and discussing the art of speaking. They were passionately interested in how language works on the listener. What were the properties of a powerful and effective speech? How could young students be taught to deliver a speech that would win the hearts and minds of an audience? The ancient Greek world

INTRODUCTION

was on fire with speaking, and crowds flocked to the plays of Sophocles and Aeschylus and rushed to hear the "rock star" orators of the day, like Lysias, Demosthenes, and Isocrates.

Words mattered to the Greeks. They were concerned not only with *what* was said, but, more importantly perhaps, with *how* it was said. So they conceived a theory of public speaking that culminated in the birth of rhetoric. Derived from the Greek word *rhetorike*, the civic art of public speaking, rhetoric is **the art of persuasion by words**, to cite Aristotle's famous definition. More specifically, as literary historian George Kennedy has noted, rhetoric focuses on the **power of words to influence a situation**. Wherever the public gathers—in courts of law, in political assemblies, in theaters, in churches, on street corners—there is an opportunity for a speaker to be persuasive and influence a situation.

Most scholars agree that a young Will Shakespeare received, at the Stratford Grammar School, a rich diet of rhetorical training directly linked to the education his Greek and Roman counterparts received centuries earlier. (Where else would he have received such regimented formal training?) It was an intensive immersion in classical Latin works: daily recitals of epistles, odes, and swashbuckling epic poetry, as well as speech composition and imitation of classical verbal styles. Above all, he learned hundreds of intoxicating verbal patterns designed to capture the ear of the audience. Like other Elizabethan playwrights, he would artfully construct speeches and dialogue employing these *devices* or *figures*. Actors were trained to recognize and exploit them in speaking on stage. These verbal patterns are laced throughout his plays, the plays of most pre-20th-century playwrights, and the dialogue of verbally attuned contemporary playwrights.

What were these devices or *rhetorical figures* (i.e., *figures of speech*) and how did actors use them in their performances? Does it have any relevance to performers today? We start with this basic premise:

> **What you cannot see in a text you cannot use as a performer.**

Awareness is the starting point. Actors in past centuries were trained to spot verbal patterns in a text and exploit them in performance. Today's actor has never received training in mining the *verbal surface*, to borrow a phrase from

INTRODUCTION

Renaissance scholar and theorist Richard Lanham. So s/he relies on the strong attributes of 20th-century actor training: *sub*text, personalization, intention, and behavioral analysis. But rhetorical figures—mesmerizing verbal patterns that provide a kind of spark or jolt to a sentence or speech—do not live beneath the text. As we have begun to see, **they live on the surface**. The orchestrated words come alive when spoken aloud.

There are hundreds of rhetorical figures in the English language. Some are brief, while others gather force across an entire speech. Their purpose was to send a thrilling *charge* into the speech, a *persuasive jolt*, sparking our ability to listen and follow the speaker's point of view. In Shakespeare's day, schoolkids knew several hundred figures. Today students know none. Actors have lost a major tool in understanding motive and in expressing text. Once a major pillar of Western education, rhetoric today has somehow come to imply empty talk, shallow communication, verbal phoniness. It is seen as a mask that covers the truth rather than an art that can help shape and express it.

It is time to rediscover the lost art of persuasive speaking and apply it to our contemporary stage—and our wild eclectic contemporary energy. Actors are hungry for new tools. They crave new ways of analyzing and performing a text.

This book examines supercharged verbal patterns, examining classical text as an important foundational source; at the same time this book has a particular interest in applying rhetorical training to *verbally adventurous contemporary plays*, where language helps create character. There are many contemporary plays featuring "heightened text" or "charged language." Words matter in these plays because they shape motive, influence the listener, and reveal personality. The chapters in this book track the ways in which spoken verbal patterns achieve their power or persuasive punch: some patterns create dramatic tension via **balance**; some passages bombard the listener with an exciting barrage of **amplification**; some use **descriptive** devices to paint graphic visual imagery; some hypnotize listeners by employing **repetitive** mantras; and others use **metaphor** to reveal wondrous new connections in the world.

All of these rhetorical devices prefer a bold, expressive—sometimes outrageous—approach to speaking, one that often overwhelms the narrowly defined vocal borders of subtext-based "realistic" dialogue.

INTRODUCTION

Language-driven actor training greatly expands an actor's expressive range on stage, specifically through the voice and the act of speaking. The "persuasive" actor is one who sends a thrilling "charge" into the language, fearlessly using sound, a propulsive sense of rhythm, and extraordinary pitch range as part of her arsenal. More importantly, perhaps, he uses fully charged speaking and dynamic vocal delivery to reveal and intensely express the character's driving desires and yearnings.

The art of rhetoric can add powerful new tools to the contemporary actor's repertoire of more commonly tapped resources, namely the use of subtext and psychological investigation of character. The 20th century brought subtle personalization to the craft of acting, inner exploration of motive and behavior, sincere investigation of a character's emotional life, which will always be part of the actor's toolbox. This approach governs the acting styles in the film and television worlds and much of the contemporary theater. But it is one style among many. It works well for some plays but seems to seriously constrain the actor in verbally adventurous texts.

The 21st century may be an era where performers can combine the psychological and rhetorical approaches, fuse the best of both worlds. Such a collaboration may be ripe as there are hopeful signs that we are beginning to wake from our long verbal malaise: exciting new playwrights are beginning to experiment with colorful dialogue; colleges are hosting Poetry Slam contests; Spoken Word and Hip-Hop theater are evidence of an emerging hunger for verbal expression. Our society may be on the verge of rediscovering the persuasive power of crafted, impassioned speech.

Today's actor is in a unique position to ride the winds of change and carry forth the blazing torch of the Speaker. The orators of yesterday are gone. Students no longer recite the *Iliad* in the classroom. Some old-school preachers still hold high the tradition of thunderous persuasion, but actors remain disconnected from this proud and vital verbal tradition, a tradition that gave birth to the Western theater several thousand years ago.

Today, young acting students study Voice and they study Speech and sometimes Shakespearean Blank Verse. All worthwhile and necessary, of course, but these subjects do not directly cover the ***art of speaking***. Vocal development, speech training, and metrical analysis can give strong muscle and backbone to the act of speaking, but they should not be confused with

INTRODUCTION

the act itself. They are key tributaries to the Big River of Speaking. It was the special province of rhetoric that provided that core training for centuries.

Think about it. In a pre-electronic age, with no boom mics, no dazzling light cues or extravagant scenery, Shakespeare's actors held the stage for over two hours, as a rowdy and raucous crowd pressed forward. What powered that kind of theater? Who supplied the electricity?

If you have been intimidated by heightened language, cheer up: this book seeks to give you some courage. If you want to be a truly versatile actor, one who can play a wide variety of styles and roles, you must learn to master the basic properties of dramatic verbal craft—in both "classical" and contemporary plays. If you are a director, you may want to arm yourself with new tools for understanding the spoken word, enabling you to guide your actors to more impactful speaking. If you are an active citizen hungry for compelling verbal expression, read on. Rhetorical craft is the key that unlocks the door.

The bold journey lies ahead. Prepare for an adventure—and let's begin.

Chapter One

STRETCHING THE TEXT:
Balance

If you loosen a string on a guitar it will eventually go slack and produce no sound. As you turn the tuning peg the string loses its tension, its energy, and sinks silently onto the guitar. It is no longer held aloft between two points: the headstock and the tailpiece. Conversely, by ratcheting the tuning peg in the opposite direction, the string begins to awaken as it becomes taut. With the increasing "stretch" comes the ability to vibrate and make sound. Stretched tightly between two points the string suddenly comes alive with sound. The guitarist can now make some music.

Language works in the same way. It craves a dynamic *stretch* between two points. When language is stretched, it has the amazing ability to reveal powerful images, ideas, arguments, contrasts. The words suddenly become vibrant because the listener can hear strong *distinctions* in the speech. The words now grab the listener by the collar. Gone is the humdrum monotone that habitually numbs our listening and sedates our speaking.

In the art of rhetoric, word stretch is often achieved through *balance*. One sequence of words is *balanced* against another sequence. There are many rhetorical figures that feature various forms of balance. A *figure* is any orchestrated verbal pattern or strategy that captures the ear of the audience. The pattern is both playful and intoxicating, as it creates a kind of electric spark, drawing the listener into the story. For actors studying rhetorical balance, there are three figures that are especially useful for performance: **Antithesis, Hypophora,** and **Deliberatio**. These are fancy classical terms for supercharged verbal figures that create balance.

All three, in different ways, require vocal stretch.

Chapter One

ANTITHESIS
Call and Response

Like many classical rhetorical names, **Antithesis** (an TITH e sis) derives from the ancient Greek language and it means "opposites." Here's a good practical definition, adapted from John Barton, for stage performers: ***The actor plays one word or phrase off another word or phrase***. Antithesis is a giant figure in the world of the spoken word. It casts its large shadow everywhere in pre-20th-century plays and in many verbally hip contemporary plays. Learning to recognize—and use—antithesis is probably the single most important step today's actor can take to boost one's verbal power.

Standing before 200,000 people gathered before the Lincoln Memorial on a sweltering August day in 1963, the Reverend Dr. Martin Luther King, Jr. unleashed an antithesis for the ages, one that still echoes and resonates today.

> I have a dream that my four little children will one day live in a nation where they will not be judged by the color of their skin but by the content of their character.
>
> ("*I have a dream*" speech, Washington, D.C., August 28, 1963)

If you speak this sentence aloud, its "call and response" structure will reveal itself.

Clearly, *content of their character* is playing off *color of their skin*. The two points or ideas are stretched emphatically apart:

color of skin   vs.   **content of character**

These two points are distinct, miles apart, radically different. Between these two points, Dr. King sets up his string of tension. Remember, in 1963, a "whites only" sign still hung in many American establishments—and cast its shadow over many more. Dr. King needed to find a compelling response to that sign, one that would provide an unassailable counterpunch. It had to have the right *sound*. Vocally and intellectually, *content of character* was a booming response to *color of skin*.

STRETCHING THE TEXT: Balance

Now let's look at a dynamic range of examples, from classical and contemporary plays—and explore how the actor can harness antithesis in performance. We'll start with a straightforward one from Shakespeare's *Macbeth*. Realizing that her husband has lost his appetite for murdering the king, Lady Macbeth attacks his "green and pale" character, then lashes his crumbling resolve with a potent verbal whip.

> Art thou afeard
> To be the same in thine own act and valor
> As thou art in desire?
>
> (1.7)

Speak this sentence aloud several times. Launch the words boldly into the space around you. What do you hear? Any word or phrase playing off another word or phrase? After trying out this sentence in several different ways, you may find some "tension" between two sections:

act and **valor**   vs.   **desire**

Lady Macbeth is making a distinction between *doing* things and *wishing* for things. She asks him, are you courageous enough to match your *actions* to your *wishes*? It's a direct challenge. Macbeth wants to be king but, like the poor cat in the adage who wants to catch fish but isn't willing to get its paws wet, he is afraid to take action. Keeping in mind our earlier guitar string analogy, let's illustrate it this way:

act and valor_____**desire**

With "act and valor" on one end and "desire" on the other, Lady Macbeth frames the necessary stretch. Put another way, the sentence has an inherent balance. "Act" (as in action) and "valor" (as in courage) are set against mere "desire." Men of action are equated with valor. Manhood. Desire, on the other hand, if not backed by deeds, is equated with weak wishing, even cowardice. How can the actor exploit this tension, that is, how can she maximize the difference between these two behaviors so that Macbeth—in his gut—feels the full force of her *persuasion*? How can she make a strong distinction

Chapter One

between bold men of action and wishful daydreamers? By ***stretching the text***. By vocally stretching "act and valor" away from "desire."

The performer has several key vocal tools with which to stretch language and thereby make strong distinctions:

◊ **Inflection (pitch)**
◊ **Stress (accent)**
◊ **Volume**
◊ **Rhythm**
◊ **Passion to Communicate**

Inflecting the voice, or playing with pitch change, empowers actors to bounce one word off another word. Listen to children at the playground. They fearlessly stretch language so that their all-important vital needs are left in no doubt: "Hey Tommy, I want the *Ninja super sword* not the *wimpy squirt gun*!" The key words soar high and dip low in pitch, answering one another. The Ninja super sword sounds very different than the squirt gun. Try this sentence out loud, have fun with it. Not in this child's wildest dream does the ninja sword occupy the same vocal pantheon as the squirt gun. They are stretched apart.

Children also love using **Stress** and **Volume** to highlight their distinctions. They instinctively accent the operative phrases or words: "I don't like *carrots*, I just wanna eat *cheese puffs*!" A child wants the adult listener to be absolutely clear about his preference. "Carrots" might be muttered firmly under the breath, while "cheese puffs" explodes with delight off the tongue. They are stretched apart.

Rhythmically, the child might choose to slow the tempo on "carr-ots" while increasing speed on "cheese puffs," thus evoking disgust at the former and exultation at the latter. Or vice versa, depending on the accompanying attitude. Children are not afraid of "overacting," they are not afraid of sound, they are not afraid of communicating. One can begin to understand in classical times why children, starting at eight or nine years of age, began to learn sophisticated and exciting rhetorical techniques of expression. It makes perfect sense: Kids have a natural affinity for communicating through sound.

This leads us to the final tool: **Passion to Communicate**. More mindset than technique, the passion to communicate one's story lies at the heart of vocal expression. Think about an episode in your life when you were filled

STRETCHING THE TEXT: Balance

with exhilaration, fully alive. Add to this memory the intense desire to share this experience by describing and communicating it so clearly and effectively that a listener vicariously experiences it as well. Shakespeare's characters can't wait to unleash some wondrous image, some fabulous account, some incredible emotion or insight. Every stage moment for them is exhilarating, even the tragic one. Like racehorses straining at the gate, they are eager to burst forth with a piece of communication that utterly captivates you.

So the passion to communicate requires extraordinary commitment to storytelling—and to the full range of vocal expression that accompanies it. When you begin to understand this desire—and it is a process of intrepid discovery—you will find that you rather naturally begin to expand your pitch range, your sense of vocal accent, volume, rhythm, your adventurousness with words. You begin to pluck out and stretch antithetical pairings so that the listener can be affected by them.

It is important to note that *stretching the text* does not imply that all words in the speech are stretched—only the *operative* ones, the specific words creating the antithesis. Otherwise the speech can roar empty bombast, or worse, highlight words that actually impede the meaning:

> Art **thou afeard**
> To be the **same** in thine own act and valor
> As **thou** art in desire?

Good luck making sense of that interpretation. Personal pronouns are not operative here, nor are words like "afeard" or "same." They can smother the antithesis with ill-informed stress and accents. Emphasizing them distracts the ear. It is therefore crucial to track down or highlight only the operative phrases—the key words that feature antithetical stretch. Therein lies the very power of rhetorical balance.

> **Remember, the alternative to stretching the text is the dull gray middle where all words are equally bland.**

No stretch. No balance. The two ends sit in the lifeless middle. "Act and valor" sound just like "desire." No way to tell them apart. The imaginary "string" between them sits limp and contracted, incapable of sound. There is

5

Chapter One

no persuasive reason that Macbeth, or the audience, should be affected by the contrast. Much of contemporary American culture celebrates a kind of monotone speaking, as it conveys a cool persona, one unfazed by the daily exigencies of life. Coolness is somehow equated with the total absence of vocal exertion, since the person is too cool, apparently, to expend the uncool energy necessary to make melodramatic verbal distinctions. The magical verbal exuberance of the child years drains away and gets replaced by the jaded vocal reluctance of the young adult years.

This attitude has a profound impact on contemporary actor training. Young actors come to believe that anything outside the narrow naturalistic box is overacting. It's phony. Not believable. So they take language brimming with exciting possibilities and flatten it into a numbing sameness. Let's break open this box and look at some more examples of how antithetical stretch works.

Double Antithesis

No playwright loved rhetorical balance more than George Bernard Shaw, whose contrarian view of the world prompted him to set radical ideas against conventional ones. In *Major Barbara*, a play that pits practical worldly power against spiritual power, the munitions maker Andrew Undershaft delivers a sermon on how the sword is mightier than the pen.

> Vote! Bah! When you vote, you only change the names of the cabinet. When you shoot, you pull down governments, inaugurate new epochs, abolish old orders and set up new.
> (Act 3)

A wicked double antithesis. The primary stretch is between "vote" and "shoot." The secondary tension is between the results of these two primary activities, namely, a reshuffling of cabinet names versus pulling down governments and ushering in new systems. We can diagram it:

STRETCHING THE TEXT: Balance

VOTE_____SHOOT

primary stretch

↓   ↓

change cabinet names_____**pull down governments**
　　　　　　　　　　　　　　　　　　　　　　　　inaugurate new epochs
　　　　　　　　　　　　　　　　　　　　　　　　abolish old orders
　　　　　　　　　　　　　　　　　　　　　　　　set up new

secondary stretch

Notice that four items gang up against only one item. Antithesis need not be symmetrical. And it need not involve opposites, it simply requires two sets of words to be held in tension. If you speak this passage aloud you will notice that the speech hangs on **VOTE** and **SHOOT**—and so the stretch between them has to be daring enough to feed the consequences: MORE OF THE SAME, on one end, and REVOLUTION on the other end. The actor playing Undershaft can strongly communicate this radical idea by inflecting or stressing these contrasting phrases, as "shoot" *calls back* to "vote."

The REVOLUTION side of the equation *responds* to the MORE OF THE SAME side. Try it. Be bold. Let the operative words "bounce off" each other. Like two opposing players smacking a tennis ball across the net, words can also be bandied back and forth, as a strong *serve* is countered with an equally strong *return of serve*.

Original illustration by artist Arielle Jessop.

Chapter One

This image may help you to find the "call and response" nature of antithetical stretch. More intriguingly, the tennis image may spur you to discover the playfulness of rhetorical language. The crafted dialogue embodies a kind of game where ideas or images compete with one another.

Fifty years after Andrew Undershaft delivered his sermon on Voting and Shooting in *Major Barbara*, another radical, Miss Cecily, championed a similar slash-and-burn strategy in Tom Stoppard's wildly polemical rollercoaster, *Travesties*. A hardcore Marxist, Cecily scoffs at society's "intellectuals" and "piecemeal reformers," declaring that change will never come from such reformers, but from a "*head-on collision.*" You cannot fix a broken system, she declares, you can only burn it down and start over. To illustrate this brazen antithesis, she unleashes an absurdly zealous anecdote about the King of Head-On Collision, Vladimir Ilych Lenin.

> When Lenin was 21 there was famine in Russia. The intellectuals organized relief—soup kitchens, seed corn, all kinds of do-gooding with Tolstoy in the lead. Lenin did—nothing. He understood that the famine was a force for the revolution.
>
> (Act 2)

Stoppard is a genius in mixing shocking diatribe with absurd humor. A ravaging famine has come to Russia, killing thousands. The bourgeois ***intellectuals*** organized humane *relief* programs—while ***Lenin*** did *nothing*. Again, a double stretch:

REFORMERS	**REVOLUTIONARIES**

Intellectuals — relief
   soup kitchens
   seed corn
   all kinds of do-gooding
   with Tolstoy in the lead
	Lenin — nothing

Look at this stunning contrast. Fourteen words describe the collective charitable activities of the intellectuals—while one empty word devastatingly reveals the brutal cunning of Lenin. When we realize that Cecily intends

STRETCHING THE TEXT: Balance

this anecdote as high praise for Lenin's revolutionary vision, we shudder at the savage irony of her antithesis. Cecily marvels at Lenin's insight that such a catastrophe would help bring in the new communist society. The famine is a means to achieve the "head-on collision" she so values. Now, the actor speaking these lines has to be unapologetically outrageous in stretching this text:

Intellectuals organized relief—soup kitchens, seed corn, all kinds of do-gooding...

LENIN did_____**NOTHING**!

"Lenin" has to bounce hard off of "intellectuals" because these two words are separated by a wide canyon of other words. Likewise, "nothing" must come as a thunderous response to "soup kitchens, seed corn, and all kinds of do-gooding." The actor can open up with all eight cylinders, sparking changes in pitch, stress, volume, and rhythm. Above all, the actor playing this part must have a take-no-prisoners *passion to communicate* the difference between Lenin and the deluded intellectuals. She must persuade Henry Carr, the person to whom she is speaking—and she must persuade us. Political zealots do not live in the world of casual mumbling indistinct conversation. They believe in the power of words to change history and so they slice and shape their communication accordingly.

Stressing or inflecting operative words is not a dry didactic rule meant to hamper the actor's sense of exploration. By all means please explore the text. *But remember that crafted language is the vehicle that shapes—and conveys—the character's intentions.* Composed language, like composed music, has a carefully orchestrated design, a deliberate strategy that performers can use to vividly express the character's thoughts and aspirations. Mozart indicated the use of *Forte* for a certain group of notes and *Pianissimo* for another group. He would answer one melody with a countermelody, releasing an exchange of "ideas." The effect created balance, a strategy that captured our listening and accented the main motifs.

The art of crafted speaking will not steal your soul, robbing you of spontaneity. Quite the contrary, it will give you more impulses and freedom to choose—among a wide range of options—how best to detonate the charges

9

Chapter One

within the text. It will broaden your expressiveness. When you speak only from Habit, you are not free because you are not aware of other options. You fall into predictable patterns that compromise spontaneity. When you suddenly see the verbal craft and its speaking clues, you can then *use* it.

Cascading Antithesis

Sometimes a speaker develops a whole *series* of statements on one side of the antithetical net, as it were, which are then answered by another series on the opposite side. It's a cascade of opposing ideas or images, first on one side ("call") and then matched on the other side ("response"). In Charles Mee's wildly intriguing play, *Big Love*, a contemporary retelling of Aeschylus' *The Suppliant Women*, fifty Greek brides escape to a manor in Italy, refusing marriage to their fifty cousins. However, the fifty grooms-in-waiting track them down and alight at the manor. Two of them, in a raucous scene packed with masculine angst, discuss women, with the experienced Constantine offering some gender tutoring to the naïve and frustrated Nikos.

> Girls are socialized
> so they want a man to be older
> take charge
> have money
> have status
> while they play hard to get
> and boys are taught to feel stupid
> feel inferior
> not as smart as girls
> then hormones happen
> a boy wants a girl
> she plays hard to get
> so a boy learns to
> talk big
> develop a line
> take all the risk
> hit on women

> not take the answer no
> look for younger women
> go for status jobs
> how do the women
> handle men like this?
> they get more hostile
> more aloof
> they wear high heels
> they diet too much
> they hate themselves
> they blame the men
> the men hate them
> it's a vicious circle
> it's a vicious circle

Notice how the pairings cascade and match each other, along the antithetical divide:

Girls:
- want a man to be older
- take charge
- have money
- have status
- while they play hard to get

Boys:
- taught to feel stupid
- feel inferior
- not as smart as girls
- then hormones happen

Then, after the antithetical pairing, "a boy wants a girl/she plays hard to get," Constantine offers more elaboration:

Men:
- learn to talk big
- develop a line
- take all the risk
- hit on women
- not take the answer no
- look for younger women
- go for status jobs

Women:
- get more hostile
- more aloof
- wear high heels
- diet too much
- hate themselves
- blame the men

Chapter One

It is important that the speaker let the audience know, vocally and rhythmically, when he has "crossed over" to the other side. It should have the sound of "that's what the **boys do**, now let's see what the **girls do**." It helps line up the opposing ideas in the audience's mind. The cascading ideas should respond vocally to one another, injecting wit and clarity to Constantine's argument. After the series on men's behavior, the playwright cleverly sets up the response with "how do the women/ handle men like this?" This question prepares our ear for the other half of the antithesis and cues the actor for the "crossover."

Outrageous Uses

Perhaps the most outrageous display of antithetical gunfire in Western literature occurs during the "Don Juan in Hell" interlude from Shaw's masterpiece, *Man and Superman*. Don Juan and the Devil are enjoying a furiously fascinating debate on the nature of Man. Rejecting Don Juan's description of his converts as weak-willed "wretched creatures," the Devil accuses Don Juan of being uncivil. Don Juan counters:

> Pooh! Why should I be civil to them or to you? In this Palace of Lies a truth or two will not hurt you. Your friends are all the dullest dogs I know. They are not beautiful: they are only decorated. They are not clean: they are only shaved and starched. They are not dignified: they are only fashionably dressed. They are not educated: they are only college passmen. They are not religious: they are only pewrenters. They are not moral: they are only conventional. They are not virtuous: they are only cowardly. They are not even vicious: they are only "frail." They are not artistic: they are only lascivious. They are not prosperous: they are only rich. They are not loyal, they are only servile; not dutiful, only sheepish; not public spirited, only patriotic; not courageous, only quarrelsome; not determined, only obstinate; not masterful, only domineering; not self-controlled, only obtuse; not self-respecting, only vain; not kind, only sentimental; not social, only gregarious; not considerate,

only polite; not intelligent, only opinionated; not progressive, only factious; not imaginative, only superstitious; not just, only vindictive; not generous, only propitiatory; not disciplined, only cowed; and not truthful at all: liars every one of them, to the very backbone of their souls.

(Act 3)

This unrelenting verbal barrage is a bravura performance piece! An over-the-top parody of antithesis. How long can Don Juan keep creating these balanced one-liners? How long can the actor keep finding distinct ways to stretch—and build—each pairing? This bombastic speech is an amazing challenge. Cardiovascularly, it is like running the 10K race. The performer needs to control breath and pace. The speech revs up like a roadster heading for the finish line. It is important to control the speed or pacing so that the performer doesn't "blow a gasket" in the first few lines. At the same time, each pairing needs distinction and stretch. The speech forces the performer to explore wider avenues of expression. Inflection, stress, volume, and rhythm are kicked into full power mode.

Try this speech when you are feeling brave and Herculean. You will gain new acting muscles and you will be rewarded for your efforts. Don't worry if the piece sounds weak, mechanical, or monotonous when you first begin. Little by little, in fits and starts, you will begin to shape it and make it catch fire.

One of the great things about formal antithetical stretch is that there is no single way to achieve this goal. There are a multitude of ways to bounce *virtuous* off *cowardly*, or *moral* off *conventional*. That's why high-voltage verbal training opens up the personality and asks the performer to keep exploring a wider and more colorful range of expression. Each performer can bring his own unique take to the speech, her own strategy of how best to communicate its wit, wisdom, and wonder. The stretch must be present, but the methods are many.

For centuries antithesis was the cornerstone of rhetorical training for young citizens, orators, lawyers, and performers, a beacon that illuminated and clarified what was vitally at stake in a given speech or written text. Today, we can reclaim this device and pass it on.

Chapter One

HYPOPHORA
Two Voices

In the Garden of Eden, Eve encounters the wily Serpent who tempts her to taste of the forbidden fruit. Eve has been warned, by God and his angels, not to taste of that particular fruit, whose sweet flavor imparts the knowledge of good and evil. Death, she is told, is the penalty for tasting it. Though she has no experience of Death, Eve senses it is a ghastly thing, certainly something to be avoided. In John Milton's epic poem, *Paradise Lost*, the Serpent must remove Eve's fear of God's warning and must persuade her to transgress a powerful commandment. The Serpent implores Eve not to believe God's "rigid threats" of Death. She shall not die with that first succulent bite.

> How should ye?—by the fruit? It gives you Life
> To knowledge. By the Threatener? Look on me,
> Me who have touched and tasted, yet both live,
> And life more perfect have attained than Fate
> Meant me, by venturing higher than my Lot.
>
> (Book IX, lines 684–688)

The Serpent speaks convincing words that pour into her ear. Not only has the Serpent not died by tasting the fruit, it has attained the remarkable gift of speaking, rational discourse, something no other animal can claim. The Serpent, in fact, has ventured *higher* than its "lot" by partaking of the fruit. Milton knew words were dangerous, that words were a double-edged sword, capable of inspiring and damning by alternate turns. So he gave his Tempter a heady verbal formula, *hypophora*, with which to win over Eve.

Hypophora (hy PO pho ra) is a ***strategy where the speaker poses a question and then immediately answers it, using two "voices."*** It is a Q&A session where the speaker asks a question in order to set up his ready answer. It is another figure of balance: "Q" on one side of the fence, "A" on the other side. When repeated in successive waves, the question-and-answer formula is diabolically persuasive, since the speaker has foreseen possible objections—in

STRETCHING THE TEXT: Balance

the question—and provides "solutions" in the answer. Look at the Serpent's potent use of the Q&A format:

Q	A
How should ye [die]—by the fruit?	It gives you life to knowledge
By the Threatener?	Look on me, me who have touched and tasted, yet both live, and life more perfect have attained...

While antithesis required vocal stretch in the previous section, hypophora requires *personality* stretch, as well as vocal distinction. Let's explain. What happens when a person controls both the question and the answer? Why is it so effective in gaining our assent as listeners? The speaker, in essence, divides oneself into two voices, two personas. It's as if she is representing the opposing party as well as herself. The speaker raises the enemy's argument—and then debunks it. Old-school lawyers knew how to use this figure to convince a jury of a client's innocence. They would anticipate the prosecution's points and deftly answer them utilizing the Q&A format. It's a neat psychological trick, one that the classical world employed quite often. For performers, it's a great opportunity to pull two "characters" out of one. We can draw it:

Warning Voice   Seductive Voice

Here the Serpent embodies the warnings of God's angels as well as its own seductive counter-responses. So the actor must stretch the two "voices" or personalities apart. One way, technically, to achieve a strong stretch is to differentiate a question from an answer. This sounds obvious until you realize how many actors make questions out of answers and answers out of questions. "My name is John Smith?" Or the opposite: "Can you give me the money." Today, many performers cannot sharply cut away an answer from a question. The vocal inflections are nearly identical (remember the dull gray middle where words lose vitality) and therefore no stretch can be achieved. Instead of two personalities, only one voice emerges and the strategy of hypophora is lost. When questions sound like answers, there can be no balance.

Chapter One

The power of hypophora is triggered when one distinct voice immediately answers another distinct voice.

A magical persuasion is suddenly present in the room.

Setup and Payoff

A variation on the strategy of two voices occurs when the speaker sets up a question and then delivers the payoff. In old-time vaudeville comedy routines, there was the "straight man" whose job was to *set up* the wisecracking jokester who would provide the punch line *payoff.* While there is no particular requirement for humor, hypophora also features this setup-payoff formula, one that allows the speaker to split himself into two characters and engage in a kind of prearranged debate. It's a prearranged or orchestrated debate because the speaker controls both the questions and answers, hoping to score points by slamming the questions with hard-hitting unassailable answers.

In Shakespeare's *Henry IV Part 1*, the wonderfully roguish reprobate Falstaff seizes on hypophora to weasel out of military service. His pal Prince Hal expects him to fight in the battle against Hotspur's forces. Honor—a big word in Elizabethan England—is at stake. Falstaff then examines this concept, Honor, wondering if it can repair an injured body on the battlefield.

> Can honor set a leg? No. Or an arm? No. Or take away the grief of a wound? No. Honor hath no skill in surgery then? No. What is honor? A word. What is in that word honor? What is that honor? Air. A trim reckoning! Who hath it? He that died a' Wednesday. Doth he feel it? No. Doth he hear it? No. 'Tis insensible then? Yea, to the dead.
>
> (5.1)

Falstaff's ingenious wit cleverly slices apart Honor and plays with it. He employs two voices to help him reduce honor to a mere breath of air. One voice embodies the "Naïve Schoolboy" while the responding voice plays the "Cynical Sage":

STRETCHING THE TEXT: Balance

NAÏVE SCHOOLBOY	CYNICAL SAGE
Can honor set a leg?	No.
Or take away the grief of a wound?	No.
What is honor?	A word.
What is that honor?	Air. A trim reckoning!
Who hath it?	He that died a' Wednesday.
Doth he feel it?	No.
Doth he hear it?	No.
'Tis insensible then?	Yea, to the dead.

There's not much left of Honor after Falstaff is through with it. The "straight man" of Schoolboy is hammered by the "jokester" of Sage. Experience responds to Innocence. With each passing Q&A combo, Falstaff gains momentum, as his two voices cut in and out, switching masks, donning different attitudes. He, of course, concludes that he will have nothing to do with Honor: He will not fight. For the audience to fully receive the impact of this kind of language, the actor must be courageous enough to distinguish the setup from the payoff. This is not only a technical challenge, involving vocal distinctions, but a "character" or role-playing challenge as well. Each separate voice is a separate persona or role.

Protagonist and Antagonist

One of the most stunning and remarkable uses of hypophora occurs near the end of Shakespeare's *Richard III*. After murdering his way to power, Richard prepares to meet the forces of an opposing army. The night before the fateful battle, he finds himself alone in his tent, wracked by nightmares. He awakes with a jolt.

> Cold fearful drops stand on my trembling flesh.
> What do I fear—myself? There's none else by.
> Richard loves Richard, that is, I am I.

Chapter One

> Is there a murderer here? No. Yes, I am.
> Then fly. What, from myself? Great reason why—
> Lest I revenge. What, myself upon myself?
> Alack, I love myself. Wherefore?—for any good
> That I myself have done unto myself?
> O no! Alas, I rather hate myself
> For hateful deeds committed by myself.
> I am a villain. Yet I lie, I am not.
>
> (5.3)

A thrashing paranoid speech, Richard unleashes several competing "voices" that vie for his tormented attention. The jagged volleys of hypophora reveal a personality divided between two impulses. Richard accuses himself, almost like a prosecutor in a courtroom, but then switches to defend himself. He plays both antagonist and protagonist, alternately accusing and defending:

ANTAGONIST	PROTAGONIST
What do I fear—myself?	**There's none else by. Richard loves Richard.**
Is there a murderer here?	**No. Yes, I am.**
Then fly.	**What, from myself?**
What, myself upon myself?	**Alack I love myself.**
Wherefore?—for any good that I myself have done unto myself?	**O no! Alas, I rather hate myself.**
I am a villain.	**Yet I lie, I am not.**

Back and forth the delirious cross-examination goes. In this particular use of hypophora, the speaker is not so much trying to anticipate objections or to play with a setup-payoff format, but rather he is wrestling with two competing visions of himself. It's a magnificent acting vehicle, allowing the performer to quickly switch from one self to another, donning one mask, tossing it away, and then donning another mask. The switches are sharp, with no transitions to blur or mitigate the schizophrenic theatricality. Notice how

Richard inverts the order of hypophora to A&Q in the antagonist's answer: "Then fly." Followed by the question: "What, from myself?"

Try this speech out loud. Play with it. It's like being on a fiendish roller-coaster, dipping down, soaring up, swerving at unexpected moments. To hang on to this ride, you have to throw away your "realistic" safety belt and let the language guide you and inspire you. Let yourself go. Uncage your voice and let it careen around the room. You may be surprised by what comes out of you. You will discover a new territory of Play and Expressiveness.

Actors underestimate the ways in which the verbal construction of a piece provides clues for understanding character and motive. Richard's speech is built on a platform of hypophora, where "Q" embodies one psychological strategy and "A" embodies another. It reveals Richard's struggling self, one that he attempts to somehow reconstitute in the face of his escalating fears. In this striking speech, the hypophora demands that the actor "cut away" or stretch the antagonist from the protagonist, one self from the other, utilizing the full arsenal of inflection, rhythm, volume, and accent. The passion to communicate both selves must be at fever pitch. Otherwise, the speech can be a clanging discordant mishmash of half-understood images and voices that blur into confusion.

Contemporary Q&A

Ever the verbal craftsman, Bernard Shaw understood the persuasive power of hypophora, letting his characters reach for its magic at opportune moments. When Mrs. Warren feels compelled to justify her life decisions, in *Mrs. Warren's Profession*, she reaches for a dose of hypophora to remove doubts and bolster her convictions. Having made a successful career as a "Madam" in the world's oldest profession, she seeks to uphold and defend her actions. "Why am I independent and able to give my daughter a first-rate education, when other women that had just as good opportunities are in the gutter? Because I always knew how to respect myself and control myself." She follows this Q&A punch with another jab: "Why is Liz looked up to in a cathedral town? The same reason." Then a final knockout swing: "Where would we be now if we'd minded the clergyman's foolishness? Scrubbing floors for one and sixpence a day and nothing to look forward to but the workhouse infirmary."

Chapter One

Setup—boom! Setup—boom! Setup—kaBOOM! The payoffs explode off of the setups. The Q&A flurry produces a tone of certainty, a convincing response to potential skeptics. Hypophora leaps into the ring, as it were, ready to take on all comers. To do that, it must exude sharp surefire distinctions, without the baggage of the "emotional pauses" that are so dear to many contemporary actors. Mrs. Warren does not hesitate or ponder internal moments. The Q&A structure knows where it is going—in advance, so it is actually thwarted by pensive forms of "naturalism." Hypophora is locked in, ready to attack. Remember, she wants to convince the listener of the fundamental truth of her life. She needs the certainty of hypophora to do that. The clues for the actor are in the verbal craft: Stretch the setup away from the payoff and play the two voices.

In John Logan's Tony Award–winning play, *Red*, the obsessed artist Rothko rails at the cheap impermanence of populist contemporary art and recoils at the audacity of his apprentice, who dares to suggest that legitimate art can be popular and for "this moment." When confronted with his elitist and "meaningful" views of high art, Rothko launches into a diatribe against the safe, pleasant, comfortable society that embraces facile satisfaction.

> "Pretty." "Beautiful." "Nice." "*Fine.*" That's our life now. Everything's "fine." We put on the funny nose and glasses and slip on the banana peel and the TV makes everything happy and everyone's laughing all the time, it's all so goddamn funny, it's our constitutional right to be amused all the time, isn't it? We're a smirking nation, living under the tyranny of "fine." How are you? Fine. How was your day? Fine. How are you feeling? Fine. How did you like the painting? Fine. Want some dinner? Fine…Well, let me tell you, *everything is not fine!*
>
> (Act 2)

Rothko's Q&A strategy skewers polite society. Here, the questions interrogate the listener, knowing the answers will be a numbing predictable sameness of attitude. The outraged persona of "Q" pummels the cozy comfort of "A." The voice of "Q" dares "A" to say anything but "fine." Hypophora's two voices allow Rothko a sharp distinction, as he activates a strong setup-payoff strategy. In this excerpt, the rhythm of hypophora is especially propulsive and *tight*; that is, the answer comes right on the heels of the question. That's part of its power. A surefire certainty—without any intervening pauses—that drives to a conclusion. The more the actor can separate or stretch the indignity of "Q" from the tepidity of "A," the more the listener is ensnared by the argument.

Hypophora was a classic figure that schoolkids studied for centuries. Shakespeare and his schoolmates practiced speeches employing this figure. It allowed them to explore multiple voices and multiple "selves" in the act of speaking. In this context we can begin to see how hypophora "opens up" the personality, gives wide leeway to personal expression. For actors, this is an invaluable tool. Actors are always seeking ways to expand their character's choices and to widen the ways their characters express themselves. *Hypophora is an actor's tool par excellence.* It celebrates role-playing. When you see it in a text, use it and relish it.

DELIBERATIO
To be or not to be

Combining elements of both antithesis and hypophora is *deliberatio*, a figure playwrights have used to spike the dramatic tension of a scene or speech. **Deliberatio**, from whose Latin origin we derive the modern English word "deliberate," occurs when a **character weighs or "deliberates" various courses of action, pitting one outcome against another.** The character tosses back and forth several competing strategies of action, as s/he attempts to determine the best way forward. Although classically labeled as a technique of argument—a strategy for effective debate—deliberatio is also, by its very nature, a figure of balance. It balances one idea off another idea, often employing elements from the Q&A format of hypophora as well. Deliberatio encourages actors to make the bold dramatic distinctions that are the hallmarks of vocal stretch.

The most famous case of deliberatio in the West opens with this echoing question: "To be or not to be?" So begins Hamlet's evaluation of two possible outcomes: "Whether 'tis nobler in the mind to suffer/ The slings and arrows of outrageous fortune,/ Or to take arms against a sea of troubles,/ And by opposing end them."

Chapter One

The actor must stretch these outcomes apart. It is important to understand that deliberatio is a formula, one very familiar to Shakespeare—and to Hamlet, who was trained to see the world in balanced equations. So was Phebe, in *As You Like It*, as her *deliberation* on her sudden attraction to Ganymede demonstrates.

> Think not I love him, though I ask for him;
> 'Tis but a peevish boy—yet he talks well—
> But what care I for words? Yet words do well
> When he that speaks them pleases those that hear.
> It is a pretty youth—not very pretty—
> But sure he's proud—and yet his pride becomes him.
> (3.5)

Each line is split right down the middle, with Ganymede's faults arrayed on one side, his praises on the other. For Phebe, it's a delicious game: Should she give her heart to him—or not? These quick switches create a wonderful comedic effect as they betray Phebe's inner struggle. One can see that verbal *formulas* do not mitigate Shakespeare's power, rather they enhance it. Likewise, for contemporary actors, these oft-neglected formulas are gateways to a richer, bolder performance.

In William Congreve's brilliant Restoration comedy, *The Way of the World*, the old and lusty Lady Wishfort anticipates, with flustered excitement, the arrival of the young Sir Rowland, who is coming to call on her. With her ragged face caked with several thick layers of oily makeup, Lady Wishfort tries out several physical strategies for receiving him.

> Well, and how shall I receive him? In what figure shall I give his heart the first impression? There is a great deal in the first impression. Shall I sit?—No, I won't sit—I'll walk.—Aye, I'll walk from the door upon his entrance; and then turn full upon him.—No, that will be too sudden. I'll lie—aye, I'll lie down—I'll receive him in my little dressing room, there's a couch.—Yes, yes, I'll give the first impression on a couch.—I won't lie neither, but loll and lean upon one elbow; with one foot a little dangling off, jogging in a thoughtful way—yes—and then as soon as he appears, start, aye,

STRETCHING THE TEXT: Balance

start and be surprised, and rise to meet him in a pretty disorder—yes. O, nothing is more alluring than a levée [*rising*] from a couch in some confusion. It shows the foot to advantage and furnishes with blushes and recomposing airs beyond comparison. Hark! There's a coach!

(4.1)

A marvelous acting vehicle! With antithesis in one hand and hypophora in the other, deliberatio fuels the hysterical humor of this speech. Consumed by a flurry of deliberation, Lady Wishfort evaluates and rehearses various body postures. She knows the crucial importance of a first impression. Look at these sharp stretches and "turnarounds":

Shall I sit? **—No I won't sit—I'll walk.**
—No, that would be too sudden.
—I'll lie—aye, I'll lie down…there's a couch.
  —I won't lie neither, but loll and lean upon one elbow, with one foot a little dangling off, jogging in a thoughtful way—yes.

She concludes that "nothing is more alluring than a levée from a couch in some confusion." Lady Wishfort has employed the tactics of deliberatio to resolve her dilemma and reach a final decision. This kind of orchestrated text invites the performer to seek clues for character and motive within the language itself. In bright neon, the language begs the actor to take advantage of it.

A slightly different take on deliberatio comes from a contemporary of Lady Wishfort, Sir Loveless in John Vanbrugh's *The Relapse*, who also struggles with vexing romantic entanglements. Sir Loveless has had a history of infidelity, but during the first half of the play he manages to avoid a "relapse," staying faithful to his wife, Amanda. But by Act 3, however, Sir Loveless begins to feel strange sensations for his wife's best friend, Berinthia. So he saunters onto the stage and, in a memorable soliloquy, attempts to sort out his feelings and loyalties. He first notes all the compassionate support that his kind wife

Chapter One

has provided as she rescued him from "that black tyrant, Vice." Furthermore, she lifted him from gloomy despair without a thought for what he might give her in recompense. He continues:

> Hasn't she done this? And if she has,
> Am I not strongly bound to love her for it?
> To love her!—Why do I not love her then?
> By earth and heaven, I do!
> Nay, I have demonstration that I do:
> For I would sacrifice my life to serve her.
> Yet hold:—if laying down my life
> Be demonstration of my love,
> What is't I feel in favor of Berinthia?
> For should she be in danger, methinks I could incline
> To risk it for her service too; and yet I do not love her.
> How then subsists my proof?
>
> (3.2)

Does he love Amanda? Does he not love her? Does he love Berinthia? Or not? This conniving cad is deliberating on Love and Fidelity and comes up with a clever barometer—sacrificing his life—to gauge his love for Amanda. But there's a small problem: he realizes that he's likely to sacrifice his life for Berinthia as well. Look at these exaggerated turnarounds that leap from one side of the fence to the other:

> —To love her!   **—Why do I not love her then?**
> —By earth and heaven, I do!...
>   I would sacrifice my life to serve her.
>   **—Yet hold...What is't I feel**
>   **in favor of Berinthia?**
> —and yet I do not love her.

What to do? How to resolve this soap opera? Sir Loveless, in a moment of pure inspiration, hits upon a solution that concludes his deliberations, eases his conscience, and provides an escape hatch.

>—Oh, I have found it out.
>What I would do for one is demonstration of my love;
>And if I'd do as much for th' other,
>If there is demonstration of my friendship—
>Ay—It must be so.
>I find I'm very much her friend.

Bingo. A reassuring antithesis placates Sir Loveless' troubled soul. Sacrificing his life for Amanda demonstrates his *love*, while sacrificing his life for Berinthia demonstrates his *friendship*. He goes on to express some consternation over the power and speed of this "friendship," but he has hit upon an expedient rationalization, a much needed solution.

Stunning Uses

Deliberatio need not confine itself to the performances of centuries past. It is alive today, wherever characters entertain bold courses of action and are not afraid to make dramatic switches in behavior and language.

One of the most stunning examples of contemporary deliberatio can be found in Peter Jackson's film adaptation of J. R. R. Tolkien's epic *Lord of the Rings* trilogy. In the second part of the film trilogy, *The Two Towers*, the wily, duplicitous character of Gollum wrestles with his obsession for the *precious* Ring. He cravenly longs for the Ring, and yet desperately seeks to be free of its spell. He deliberates with his Self, switching between his corrupted half, Gollum, and his earlier identity, Sméagol, while his master (the hobbit Frodo) lies sleeping with the Ring. Gollum insults his other half, while Sméagol plays defense and drives Gollum away. Back and forth "they" go, doling self-respect and self-loathing in equal doses. Viewers of this highly successful film will attest to the radical switches of self and voice inherent in actor Andy Serkis' interpretation of the computer-generated Gollum/Sméagol. It is a tour de force performance.

Deliberatio allows a character to explore and "sound out" a range of thoughts or actions, each with its own supporting persona. It's another classic actor's device, featuring quick changes of personality and assertion. Deliberatio openly invites the actor to play and to exploit the essential theatricality of this figure.

Chapter One

TAKING STOCK

We have examined three key figures of balance in this chapter. All three figures, in different ways, ask the actor to *stretch the text*. Words or phrases are stretched, personalities are stretched, and courses of action are stretched. By stretching the text, the actor suddenly frees herself from the bondage of monotony—and empowers herself to make trenchant distinctions between one idea and another idea, between one persona or voice and another persona or voice. These three figures, as we have seen, lie lifeless when they are buried in the timid "middle." They crave an opposing pull of forces extending to the edges. Indeed, a rhetorical figure of balance awakens when it is suddenly made taut and wound tighter and tighter. That stretch enables verbal power and activates the art of persuasion.

For the actor, the vocal tools of inflection, stress, volume, rhythm, and passion to communicate are critical allies in this "stretching" process. These tools, while indispensable, are not sufficient by themselves; they require a bold, adventurous, playful, and unapologetic spirit. When the text is truly stretched, the theatrical "guitar string" that we started tuning will suddenly find its voice and speak its story.

Chapter Two

POWERING THE TEXT:
Amplification

Just as a rowdy muscle car has a high-performance transmission that kicks into increasingly higher gear on demand, so language has a series of rhetorical *figures* that "ratchet up" and amplify human communication when activated. Driving permanently in second gear would be a tedious, monotonous, nerve-wracking, inefficient, and maddening process. If you own a souped-up eight-cylinder dual-cam Mustang with six gears of driving pleasure, you would certainly want to take advantage of all six gears. That's horsepower. To "express" itself fully, with maximum results, that Mustang craves the open road, where it can unleash all of its strengths and features.

Language desires the same freedom. It relishes *amplification*. The origin of this word is traced to the Latin *amplificatio*, meaning "enlargement." This definition finds resonance in the early Greek rhetoricians, who described the ability of language to "exaggerate" or "amplify" (*auxeteon*) a piece of communication. By harnessing the amplifying properties of language, an actor allows the words to create more impact, generate more excitement, and become even more persuasive. The words also become more playful, inviting the listener to partake in the thrill of human verbal expression.

Today's actors are simply not provided with the tools of verbal amplification. They remain, for the most part, stuck in second gear, unaware that their engines can perform much more dynamically. Worse yet, actors are not particularly encouraged today to "open up the hood" and explore the mechanisms of greater verbal power on stage. Such an exploration might compromise the low-gear "realistic" dialogue that pervades so many contemporary plays. Once a vital part of every schoolkid's toolbox for centuries, the exciting figures of verbal amplification remain hidden from today's performers.

In this chapter, then, we will explore key rhetorical figures of amplification that allow the actor to power the text and shift into new gears of expression.

Chapter Two

In particular, we will examine the figures of **Accumulatio, Appositio, Auxesis,** and **Diazeugma**.

Start your engines.

ACCUMULATIO
The 0 to 60 Figure

Accumulatio (ah Koo moo LAH tee o) is likely the most high-octane and potent of amplifying figures. It means "heaping up" and our modern word "accumulation" obviously derives from this Latin predecessor. Accumulatio is a *steamrolling barrage of descriptive words or phrases that generates persuasive power.* This charging figure can go from 0 to 60 in an escalating dash. Its strategy, however, is not so much dependent on speed as on *momentum*—one that culminates in a strong exciting payoff. We might call such gathering momentum *verbal drive.*

Short-Track Accumulatio

Accumulatio can bolt into a hundred-meter sprint or it can build up over a much longer haul. For the sprint strategy, let's take a look at Henry Carr in Tom Stoppard's dazzling play of ideas, *Travesties*. Championing patriotism in war, Carr attacks the heretical Tristan Tzara, who dismisses war as a profit-based game of the rich and mighty, a form of naked capitalism. An outraged Carr counters with this one-line zinger.

> My God, you little Rumanian wog—you bloody dago—
> you jumped-up phrase-making smart alecy arty-intellectual Balkan turd!!!
>
> (Act 1)

Carr roars down the runway and doesn't let up until he's crossed the finish line. Look at this structure. The sentence amplifies, it accumulates; it escalates to a final payoff—"Balkan turd!!!" For a short track, it generates tremendous *verbal drive*. The sentence may slightly increase in speed but it primarily gathers force and power by its sheer drive. In another image, you can think of it as an escalating drum roll concluding with a resounding cymbal crash.

How can the actor really exploit the power of accumulatio on stage? For starters, eliminate all "realistic pauses" and "searching moments"—both designed to give the impression of improvised spontaneity—that blunt the verbal drive of these well-crafted amplifying structures. We can diagram it:

> My God…you little…Rumanian…wog….you bloody…dago—you jumped-up…phrase…making smart…alecy arty-intellectual Balkan……turd!!!

These searching pauses and reflective moments—so ubiquitous in contemporary realism—impede the sentence's power. We need a different strategy for this text. This language is locked in, ready to go. It's preloaded. The Carr is fueled, ready to rip. The actor steps on the pedal and uses this high-octane language to ignite the text.

The next step is to pace your breathing and sense of phrasing so that the words keep building until they cymbal crash onto "Balkan turd!!!":

> My God→you little Rumanian wog→you bloody dago →—you jumped-up→phrase-making smart alecy→arty-intellectual Balkan turd!!!

Power it. This does not mean that everything is rushed and blurred, monochromatic. Indeed, "phrase-making" is different from "smart alecy," which in turn is different from "arty-intellectual." You still need to differentiate these terms and give each a unique flavor.

Speed is not equivalent to Drive. Accumulating speeches are fueled by verbal drive, a kind of charging crescendo that soars to the summit.

Try out Carr's one-liner in full voice. It may sound forced and mechanical in your first dozen attempts. That's fine. You are learning how to play a new kind of instrument. Be patient with yourself and good results will follow. You

Chapter Two

may find that you need a quick "catch breath" after *Rumanian wog* and another one after *bloody dago*. That's OK. These quick catch breaths should not be confused with deflating pauses or pondering introspective moments. They are simply quick intakes of air (or fuel) that allow the actor to keep momentum alive.

Keeping momentum alive is really the key to accumulatio. When you steadily build the words toward a conclusion you release the persuasive power of this figure. The last section of Carr's sentence—"you jumped-up phrase-making smart alecy arty-intellectual Balkan turd!!!"—can be uttered on one breath. Try it. Audiences are captivated by the exciting structure of accumulatio. It can bring them to the edge of their seats.

Accumulatio certainly entrances the lead character of Lucy in Melanie Marnich's very inventive and quirky play, *Quake*. Lucy, on a long quest for Mr. Right, runs into a "dangerously good-looking" car mechanic, a man of almost no words, cigarette dangling from the lips, as he clangs away in his auto garage. Lucy does all the talking, describing her car's problems, as the man mutters a rare "yep" and "uh-huh." What does he think is wrong with her car? He thinks—and thinks—and then hammers out this unexpected drum roll:

> Sounds like a carburetor/crankshaft/hose/joint/nut/bolt/spark/fuel/bullshit/crap thing.
>
> (Scene 12)

"You talk!" responds an ecstatic Lucy. This short but whacky accumulating line surprises us—and her. We are not prepared for it, and it hits us right between the eyes with weird delight. This line does not have the big payoff of Henry Carr's line but it nevertheless drives forth relentlessly. The momentum of the line, spurred on by the playwright's use of slash marks, carries its full impact. From muttering grunts to an articulated fusillade of words, the playwright swings us from one extreme to another, to great effect.

One of the more exciting displays of accumulatio is featured in John Marston's satiric Elizabethan tragicomedy, *The Malcontent*. Mendoza, an insinuating court minion, full of exuberant self-flattery and preening affectation, basks in his role as a "favorite" of the duchess. He imagines himself at the center of influence, as "petitionary vassals" bow before him and palace lackeys

POWERING THE TEXT: Amplification

gaze upon his brow. But the greatest perk is his access to the ladies at court. With visions of "sweet women" wafting in his midst, Mendoza works himself into a state of mounting ecstasy with this memorable amplifying run.

> You preservers of mankind, life-blood of society. Who would live, nay, who can live without you? O Paradise! how majestical is your austerer presence! how imperiously chaste is your more modest face! but, O, how full of ravishing attraction is your pretty, petulant, languishing, lasciviously-composed countenance!
> (1.5)

These escalating phrases perfectly mirror Mendoza's delirious passion. The speech unfurls with a heated urgent tempo, building to a climax of delight.

It is an outrageous display, like the character himself, one who uses words to shape—and give titillating expression to—his wild imaginative schemes.

Try out Mendoza's speech. See if you can drive these mounting phrases to an exciting payoff.

Climbing the Staircase

In Mac Wellman's *Bad Penny*, a play where characters howl street-tough urban arias at each other, the Second Woman dissects the treacherous wiles of another woman, Kat. She begins with a staccato blast of amplification, describing Kat as:

> Vicious. Antisocial. Avaricious. Maladjusted. Possibly a drunk.
> Probably a loony tunes. Human garbage. Schemer. Tramp.
> Weirdo. Fake.

Don't be fooled by the punctuation, the parade of periods. Each adjective builds on top of the previous one, moves up a notch, as if the words are "climbing the staircase." The speaker hungers for ever more adventurous images or words, as if the previous one is not adequate by itself. Or the speaker simply needs a flurry of escalating descriptions to make her point. We can draw this "staircase":

Chapter Two

                            Fake
                        ↑ Weirdo
                      ↑ Tramp
                  ↑ Schemer
              ↑ Human garbage
            ↑ Probably a loony tunes
          ↑ Possibly a drunk
        ↑ Maladjusted
      ↑ Avaricious
    ↑ Antisocial
Vicious

These words march up the mountain, oblivious to wind or rain, eager to reach the summit. For the actor, this staircase is an invitation to climb fearlessly. Each step should be a unique declaration, a separate rung of meaning. You cannot go home again: Find a new flavor or urgency at each new level of your climb so that each new adjective sounds different from the previous one. That makes the climb interesting and it captures the ear. Monotony is always the obstacle sulking in our path. The actor must jump over it or push it out of the way.

Go ahead, climb this staircase and see if you can confidently get to the top—without losing the momentum that accumulatio requires. Give each adjective its singular flavor while allowing each word or phrase to propel you upward to the next level. This is a miniworkout but an invigorating climb. Try it out in different ways, taking a variety of approaches. Experiment with taking quick breaths at key junctures, play with your pitch and stress and volume. And play with rhythm as you wrap the speech in an exhilarating crescendo!

One of the ways the actor can avoid losing verbal drive or momentum is to abolish unnecessary vocal "downglides" or "down-endings" in one's speaking. Downglides are the vocal inflections that we typically place at the *end* of a sentence: "The dog barked at the train. ↓" It has an "I've finished" kind of sound. Finality. This sense of finality is of course necessary at the completion of a thought or sentence, but it chops a sentence into disconnected bits and pieces when placed haphazardly in the middle of a sentence: "The dog ↓ barked ↓ at the train." The sentence ends twice before it reaches its conclusion.

POWERING THE TEXT: Amplification

It has three phrases instead of only one. Contemporary spoken American English is flooded with these midsentence vocal down-endings that prevent verbal drive and are roadblocks to an amplifying run: Vicious ↓ Antisocial ↓ Avaricious ↓ Maladjusted ↓ The car cannot take off because it is constantly losing power, returning to first gear.

Vocal downglides hamper verbal drive because the sentence is constantly dying before it reaches its final destination.

The actor has several options to keep a sentence alive: upglides and level glides: The dog barked at the train ↑ (like a question) or The dog barked at the train→ (like an unfinished thought that has more to say…). Any combination of these two glides keeps a thought afloat and an amplifying run from diving into the ground. They are the technical equivalents of a passionate storyteller who insists that the punch line has not yet arrived, that the good stuff has yet to come: "Wait→here it comes→here it comes→look out!→watch out!→coming right at ya!→don't bat your eyes or you'll miss it!→BOOM! ↓" Only after reaching the summit does the thought finally conclude.

If you are really hooked into the sheer exhilaration of your story, you will find the momentum-sustaining vocalizations that propel your climb, that launch your vehicle down the highway toward a final destination.

Two Climbers

Climbing the staircase can also be accomplished by two characters that spur and push each other to the top. They "build" the staircase together. Let's look again at Melanie Marnich's play *Quake*. Brian and Lucy, in bed, are watching TV. Brian channel-surfs and stops briefly on the evening news. Lucy suddenly spots "That Woman," a strange mysterious criminal.

> LUCY: Look at her. That shot from the ATM camera. She's amazing.
> BRIAN: She's scary.
> LUCY: She's beautiful.
> BRIAN: She's a freak.

Chapter Two

> LUCY: She's a force.
> BRIAN: She's horrible.
> LUCY: She's intense.
> BRIAN: She kind of has nice eyes.
> LUCY: She's incredible. And she's out there. Somewhere.
> BRIAN & LUCY: I think I love her.
>
> (Scene 2)

A very intriguing climb. This kind of dialogue requires two characters to build momentum together, to work together rhythmically, to drive each other forward. Both actors are responsible for generating a dramatic crescendo that culminates in the payoff, "I think I love her." If either actor falls into the trap of drawn-out introspective musing, for instance, s/he can extinguish the persuasive power of this amplifying structure.

There is no single climb that is perfect or the "best" way. Even a slower pace can create amplification, as long as it drives forth with determination.

Long-Distance Accumulatio

No contemporary playwright uses amplifying figures more than Mac Wellman, whose characters inhabit the existential wastelands of a ludicrous yet frightening society imploding under industrial decay and urban alienation. His characters claw and scrape at language, trying to assemble a vision of an unfathomable world. They heap up piles of words in a frantic search for meaning.

In *Bad Penny*, a woman warns a man that he is in danger, alleging that a character named Kat and her associates are monitoring his thoughts and attempting to ensnare him in a "clandestine operation." She continues with an all-out barrage of *extended* accumulatio.

> I am your *only* friend and I have documents to prove this, documents which reveal a vast conspiracy against you, a conspiracy organized by ones close to you, family, friends, colleagues at your place of work; all their schemes center on the total destruction of you, your happiness, sanity, the health of your cat and dog and

houseplants; the destruction of your credit, reputation, your morale, your good-standing in the community, and even your self-identity and your faith in God who is over all, and who ordains all things, even vast conspiracies such as this. Do I make myself clear? Be warned.

This is a full-throttle speech. Its engine drives unrelentingly forth, kicking into all six gears, gathering force as it heads toward the finish line of "Be warned." It is the accumulated impact of this speech that grabs us, as the woman snatches images, thoughts, opinions and piles them atop one another in her desperate drive toward some ominous conclusion.

For accumulatio to unleash its energy, it needs momentum and an absence of prolonged inner pauses. Most importantly, perhaps, accumulatio requires a sense of theatricality, a larger-than-life boldness in speaking. Let's try this speech. The actor can control *verbal drive* through:

◊ **pacing**
◊ **breath control**
◊ **phrasing**
◊ **inflection**—**an avoidance of vocal downglides**

These four keys create verbal drive. So let's break this speech apart and examine one way that we might work it out, exploring the guideposts listed above:

I am your *only* friend and I have documents to prove this// →

documents which reveal a vast conspiracy against you// →

a conspiracy organized by ones close to you// →

family friends colleagues at your place of work// →

all their schemes center on the total destruction of you// →

your happiness// →

sanity// →

the health of your cat and dog and houseplants// →

> the destruction of your credit// →
>
> reputation your morale// →
>
> your good-standing in the community// →
>
> and even your self-identity and your faith in God// →
>
> who is over all and who ordains all things// →
>
> even vast conspiracies such as this// →
>
> Do I make myself clear// ↑
>
> Be warned ↓

In the schematics above, we have used a double slash mark to denote a single quick intake of *breath*. Each separate line indicates a distinct *phrase*. The level arrow mark at the end of each phrase indicates both *pacing* and *inflection*; that is, each arrow propels the speaker to the next phrase and it also maintains an "unfinished" inflection that tells of more things to come. These arrows remind us to avoid down-endings or vocal downglides—until we get to the very end of this dizzying journey—"Be warned ↓" We have purposely eliminated all punctuation marks so that we can concentrate on the unadorned structure of the language.

The above schematics are merely a guide. Training wheels, of a sort. They are only valuable to the degree that you allow them to help you move down the road. These guidelines are not substitutes for your own theatrical bravery or creative imagination. You can take the training wheels off when you feel ready to try out your own strategy for this speech. Again, there are many different strategies an actor can use. In the meantime, this technical breakdown is a good starting point.

Give this speech a test drive. You can follow the schematics or experiment with your own strategy. Where do you want to phrase and where do you want to take a quick breath? Interpretations can vary. Can you maintain sharp phrasing while pushing the speech forward? Do you occasionally sense that the speech—perhaps in the middle section—is losing its drive or power? Why did it start to downshift or lose its vitality? What about the overall goal of verbal drive? What does it take to keep momentum alive? Do you notice that any particular phrases are "diving" into the ground? All of these

POWERING THE TEXT: Amplification

considerations are vital in understanding how *long-distance accumulatio* generates its persuasive appeal and impact.

Let's take another ride, one that takes us to the dizzying edge of amplification. Long-Distance Accumulatio on Turbo Power is featured in Sarah Kane's *Crave*, a play where, at its heart, four characters—or perhaps four voices of one self—search for love, however distant or painful or unattainable. But this difficult journey is suddenly illuminated with one florid outpouring delivered by the character of "A."

> And I want to play hide-and-seek and give you my clothes and tell you I like your shoes and sit on the steps while you take a bath and massage your neck and kiss your feet and hold your hand and go for a meal and not mind when you eat my food and meet you at Rudy's and talk about the day and type up your letters and carry your boxes and laugh at your paranoia and give you tapes you don't listen to and watch great films and watch terrible films and complain about the radio and take pictures of you when you're sleeping and get up to fetch you coffee and bagels and Danish and go to Florent and drink coffee at midnight and have you steal my cigarettes and never be able to find a match and tell you about the tv programme I saw the night before and take you to the eye hospital and not laugh at your jokes and want you in the morning but let you sleep for a while and kiss your back and stroke your skin and tell you how much I love your hair your eyes your lips your neck your breasts your arse your

And the speech abruptly cuts off, hinting at more licentious interests. But then it starts up again, pursuing its breathtaking sweep and accumulation. It's as if the speaker cannot halt the momentum of this epic plea lest the frenzied passion of this relationship should suddenly vanish or fade away. Indeed, the character needs to sustain this wild rollercoaster through a driving energy that must keep going forward in order to capture the topsy-turvy multifaceted essence of the relationship. The listener is held in awe awaiting the outcome. The performer has to keep momentum alive using our four key guideposts: pacing, breath control, inflection, phrasing. And a *passion* to communicate it.

Chapter Two

Look how the speech is also supported by the repeated use of the conjunction "and," which in rhetorical terms is called *polysyndeton*—the deliberate use of conjunctions between words or phrases. In this case, the "ands" serve to generate momentum and a kind of seamless flowing continuity, adding to the overall sweep of the piece. The performer should not accent the "and," for it is simply a linking word, but rather use it to propel rhythmic swing from one phrase to the next.

All of this serves to increase the building intensity of the speech, as it heads into the homestretch, one eagerly awaited by the audience:

> ...and wander the city thinking it's empty without you and want what you want and think I'm losing myself but know I'm safe with you and tell you the worst of me and try to give you the best of me because you don't deserve any less and answer your questions when I'd rather not and tell you the truth when I really don't want to and try to be honest because I know you prefer it and think it's all over but hang on in for just ten more minutes before you throw me out of your life and forget who I am and try to get closer to you because it's beautiful learning to know you and well worth the effort and speak German to you badly and Hebrew to you worse and make love with you at three in the morning and somehow somehow somehow communicate some of the overwhelming undying overpowering unconditional all-encompassing heart-enriching mind-expanding on-going never-ending love I have for you.

This entire speech (of which this is a significant excerpt) is one sentence and it finally concludes with "love I have for you." Period. In the final exhilarating stretch, the accumulatio shifts into overdrive as the swell of adjectives increases to an exciting payoff. When you are feeling heroic, like Achilles or Andromache, try this speech. Take the journey. Stand up, look out across the remarkable landscape of this speech, take note of its distance and changes in topography, and take that first step. Keep going. You are heading into unexplored territory—and that's where the adventure and growth reside. The speech will be your loyal guide, giving you directions and clues and encouragement.

Accumulatio is a must-have tool in the contemporary actor's toolbox. We have seen how this amplifying vehicle generates tremendous verbal drive, theatrical excitement, and intensity. It requires an intrepid spirit, a performer who can infuse the technical demands of this steamrolling figure with a bursting-at-the-seams desire to relate some blazing piece of communication. It is an innately dramatic figure. Accumulatio is a potentially thrilling figure that activates the core of our ability to listen and communicate.

APPOSITIO
the Renamer

Supposing Johnny dashes into the room and excitedly proclaims: "Mary invited me to the Christmas dance!" We would feel happy for Johnny, certainly, but unless we knew Mary we might not feel the full impact of this blissful announcement. If we were to discover a little more about Mary we might gain an increased appreciation for Johnny's excitement. Supposing Johnny had exclaimed, "Mary, Prom Queen, Revlon Model, Miss Jackson County Rodeo Princess, invited me to the Christmas dance!" Wow. We now realize that Johnny is indeed blessed among men. We have received some *amplifying* information about Mary that has significantly altered the presentation of Mary—and our reaction to the news.

This particular amplifying technique, in classical times, was referred to as *Appositio*, a Latin term related to the placing of something "side by side." This concept is closely allied with an earlier Greek term, *Epexegesis*, an "explanation." So, appositio is both "explaining" and placing something "side by side." If we look at the example above, the epithets "Prom Queen," "Revlon Model," and "Miss Jackson County Rodeo Princess" are placed *side by side* with "Mary"—and they provide further *explanation* of Mary. All of the three epithets are in fact Mary:

Mary = Prom Queen = Revlon Model = Miss Jackson County Rodeo Princess

Chapter Two

The subject, Mary, is repeated over and over and over, in different ways. Notice that the epithets are not adjectives describing Mary. They *are* Mary. **Appositio** (Ap po SI ti o) *is a renaming of a person or thing or concept over and over. It offers a sharp boost of explanation in its "side-by-side" strategy.*

The act of renaming has its earliest known source in Homer's *Iliad* in which the naming of heroes and gods is bolstered by appositives or side-by-side explanations, like "Ajax, Royal Son of Telamon, Captain of Armies." This tradition was 2,000 years old by the time Shakespeare walked into the Globe Theatre. Pick up any Shakespearean play and you'll find characters that amplify a person or thing by renaming it. The Elizabethan world of Shakespeare was well versed in this technique and came to view it as an important heightening tool, a kind of light beam that illuminated the subject in megawatt power.

> **When you rename something or somebody, you are increasing its value and heightening its importance. You are *amplifying* its very essence.**

In the third part of Shakespeare's *Henry VI* cycle, which chronicles the Wars of the Roses, Lord Warwick, an emissary from King Edward of England, pays an official visit to the court of King Louis of France. He greets the French king with this opening sequence.

> From worthy Edward, King of Albion,
> My lord and sovereign, and thy vowéd friend,
> I come in kindness and unfeigned love.
>
> (3.3)

Warwick, on a diplomatic mission to unite the French and English dynasties through a marriage scheme, knows that he must portray England's king in a flattering context. Look how Edward is "explained" or renamed in Warwick's greeting:

Edward = King of Albion = my lord and sovereign = thy vowéd friend

POWERING THE TEXT: Amplification

Side by side, Edward increases in importance with each additional renaming. Again, all four terms are interchangeable in the sense that they are all the same *subject*—Edward:

My lord and sovereign = thy vowéd friend = King of Albion = Edward

Warwick's opening barrage of appositio holds us in suspense, as it were, since we do not yet know the *action* of the sentence. He ratchets up the value of Edward and finally gets to the action: "I come in kindness and unfeigned love." For the actor, appositio presents an opportunity to master ***vocal insistence***, ***drive***, and ***phrasing***.

What compulsive characteristic in human behavior or communication moves us to continually rename a person or thing? For Warwick, it is not enough to simply say, "From worthy Edward I come in kindness and unfeigned love." He needs additional amplification for Edward. Each new renaming must have a certain "wait-a-second-I've-got-an-even-better-version" quality to it. That's vocal *insistence*. It's a firm belief that the speaker needs each new epithet and is *insisting* that the picture of Edward is incomplete without each amplifying name.

Vocal insistence pushes the sentence forward as each new name hits home, builds on the previous one. It craves surplus elaboration. Insistence is the companion of verbal *drive*. They work hand in hand to put a charge into the sentence. Together, they kick the sentence forward. Indeed, appositio relies on the momentum generated by *accumulatio*. When a speaker insists on each new name s/he intuitively finds a slightly different color for each. Yes, the subject is the same, but the melody for each new name is subtly varied. Playing with vocal insistence also keeps the demons of monotony at bay. We can schematically illustrate the combination of insistence and drive:

Edward → King of Albion → my lord and sovereign → **thy vowéd friend**

In experimenting with insistence, it is important to keep pushing the speech forward toward its action. As with accumulatio, down-endings must be avoided because the speaker is "on a roll." If the speaker places vocal downglides after each name—King of Albion ↓ my lord and sovereign ↓—he

Chapter Two

loses the mounting crescendo and the power of insistence. Warwick has more to say and keeps us in suspense until the final outcome.

The final outcome or action, as indicated earlier, is Warwick's announcement that he comes in kindness and love. So his speech can be split into two sections: 1) the renaming and 2) the action:

> **From worthy Edward, King of Albion,**
> **My lord and sovereign, and thy vowéd friend,**
>
> **I come in kindness and unfeigned love.**

It is important to know the structure of this speech so that we can *phrase* it. If the actor blurs the renaming of Edward into the action, the audience is lost and cannot follow the sense of the speech. The action needs a different flavor or rhythm than the *renaming*. Another way to look at it is to phrase the renaming as one unit or whole—and then slice this unit away from the action. In our example of Mary and Johnny, we must phrase the subject, Mary (and all of her renaming), away from the action: "invited me to the Christmas dance!"

Phrasing, knowing what goes with what, is another critical component of the actor's verbal tools. Phrasing guides the actor—and the audience—into the full understanding and enjoyment of anything s/he chooses to communicate.

Subject as "Heavyweight Champion"

Sometimes a sentence consists wholly of the subject being repeated in various wild disguises, building in urgency, without any action words attached to it. All subject. It's a wonderfully suspenseful amplifying effect requiring a fun, daring use of insistence. In Eric Overmyer's play *In a Pig's Valise*, a hip nightclub DJ introduces the show's main attraction, an exotic, undulating singer-dancer named Dolores Con Leche.

> And now—accompanied by the ever-lactating Balkanettes—
> the star of our show—the filibrating thrush herself—the Hispanic Hyperventilator—Dolores Con Leche.

POWERING THE TEXT: Amplification

This strategy of incrementally "ratcheting up" the subject is the trademark style of American boxing matches, where the ring announcer teases out a string of theatrically charged "explanations" of each contender, finally culminating in the boxer's name: "In this corner, weighing in at 225 pounds, the Pride of Brooklyn, the Titan from Brighton, the Razzle Dazzle Kid, the Twisting Tornado, the Two-Time Heavyweight Champion of the World—Rocky 'Big Bubba' Caruso!" Ring announcers know how to work a crowd, how to rev them up, how to get them ready for the Big Show.

Obsessive Renaming

When a particular subject consumes a character, he often reaches for a blast of appositio to express his compulsion or addiction. The compulsive use of this side-by-side figure frequently requires the actor to rename the subject across an extended driving "run."

In Mac Wellman's *A Murder of Crows*, a play about industrial waste seeping into the homes and minds of small-town America, Howard unexpectedly releases pent-up feelings for his deceased neighbor, Raymond, at the funeral.

> I don't never forget
> nothing nobody done did to me since I was ten years
> old and this pathetic, crypto-commie, this alien
> stooge, this human farce; this rabbit-faced, luckless
> goon; this milksop; this weakling; this devious,
> evil-minded, dirty little yellow bastard;—man I wish
> I could've run him through a roaring buzz saw, or
> chuck him whole hog into a MacCormick Reaper and
> watch him spill out the other end like human spaghetti.

This speech is a manic *explanation* of Raymond and it propels headlong toward its action. Howard's obsession with Raymond is given full vent by the vehicle of appositio. Raymond is renamed seven times:

crypto-commie
stooge
farce

Chapter Two

**goon
milksop
weakling
bastard**

We have stripped away the juicy adjectives, for now, to highlight the skeletal subject. All seven terms sit side by side with Raymond, the subject. All seven terms *are* Raymond. Howard *insists* on—and relishes—each new name, amplifying Raymond in increasingly graphic colors and savage synonyms. The actor riding this dangerous wave must hang on and maintain momentum. He must keep the speech alive by insisting that each new name is vital and necessary and in fact better than the preceding name.

Notice how Howard builds tremendous *suspense* by using extended renaming. He withholds the action, which does not arrive until the final section of the speech.

>   —man I wish
> I could've run him through a roaring buzz saw, or
> chuck him whole hog into a MacCormick Reaper and
> watch him spill out the other end like human spaghetti.

So the speech contains a gathering buildup—and then it crashes onto shore with a violent action. Again, these two distinct sections need distinct phrasing. The snaking side-by-side sequence has one driving rhythm and melody, while the payoff action sequence has a different rhythm and melody.

Give this speech a road test. Try utilizing the renaming to catapult you across the language. You may lose your breath, you may stumble across the words, you may lose momentum, you may get exasperated. Good. You are discovering a sizzling new approach to speaking and communicating. Keep the faith.

Characters are consumed by *concepts* as well, as when Macbeth begins to chant about Sleep. After killing the sleeping king and his guards, Macbeth hears voices proclaiming that he shall "sleep no more." Sleep will evade him throughout the play, as he enters a hellish world of ghosts and hallucinations and paranoia. As if sensing the dear loss of this nourishing function, he begins to explain Sleep as:

POWERING THE TEXT: Amplification

> The death of each day's life, sore labor's bath,
> Balm of hurt minds, great nature's second course,
> Chief nourisher in life's feast.
> (2.2)

Each descriptive passage is Sleep. That is, Sleep is "the death of each day's life" or "balm of hurt minds." Actors are often puzzled by this kind of passage. First, many are not aware that Sleep is being repeated in various guises or, if they are aware of this, they don't understand the point of such amplifying activity. Almost embarrassed by such language, they rush through it in order to get it out of the way. But the language is the point. It provides critical clues to character. Here, the appositio is signaling a mesmerizing obsession. Use it.

The Gold Medal for the most epic and astounding use of side-by-side renaming belongs to Shakespeare's John of Gaunt in *Richard II*. On his death bed, upon hearing of the king's reckless tax-and-spend policies that threaten to bankrupt the country, the patriotic Gaunt begins to unfurl an homage to England.

> This royal throne of kings, this sceptred isle,
> This earth of majesty, this seat of Mars,
> This other Eden, demi-paradise,
> This fortress built by Nature for herself
> Against infection and the hand of war,
> This happy breed of men, this little world,
> This precious stone set in the silver sea…
> (2.1)

Gaunt is running a marathon. He is not finished, as he picks up his intensity and mounting descriptive synonyms.

> This blessed plot, this earth, this realm, this England,
> This nurse, this teeming womb of royal kings…

John of Gaunt then heads into the homestretch.

> This land of such dear souls, this dear dear land,
> Dear for her reputation throughout the world—

Chapter Two

Is now leased out—I die pronouncing it—
Like to a tenement or pelting farm.
(2.1, bold mine)

Gaunt crosses the finish line with his long-awaited conclusion: "is now leased out." The whole marathon run can be summarized thus:

England is now leased out!

Subject, action. That's it. It seems remarkably easy to percolate this entire speech down to its fundamental elements, but such is the case. Once you see how the language is heaping and renaming and twisting down the road, you can track it down. Obviously, this speech demands a driving momentum and a titanic verbal **insistence**. Otherwise, you run out of fuel before reaching your destination.

Appositio is a verbal device that speaks to strong human compulsion and elaboration. When we find a subject that utterly fascinates us, we hold it up to the light and call it by various names. This act of calling or renaming is a verbal craft that actors must rediscover. As we have seen, it provides clues for verbal drive and insistence and phrasing. Furthermore, it is a key ally in dissecting a character's state of mind. Side by side, Appositio, the Renamer, the Explainer, the Great Elaborator, the Obsessive One, tells us much about ourselves.

AUXESIS
Promethean Flame

What if you lived in a wildly playful society where everyone preferred the extraordinary word to the ordinary one? In such a world, people might use "industrial chariot" for "car," or they might ask you for a stick of "Promethean flame" instead of a "match" in order to light a candle. More subtly, people would speak of "trekking" rather than "walking," gazing at the "firmament" rather than the "sky," and, in a nod to hip slang, they would use "ripped off" for "cheated," or "chill" for "relax." On the more extreme fringes, those who fall in love would be "pierced by Cupid's shaft."

POWERING THE TEXT: Amplification

What do all of these "extraordinary" terms have in common? They ask the listener to notice words. To take delight in them. Language has a way of reawakening our impulses, making us aware of the world around us by reconfiguring it in unexpected ways. Tedious things like matches suddenly burst into new life with "Promethean flame," which links us with mythical gods and stolen fire and high drama! Suddenly, the act of lighting a candle or cigarette becomes an audacious epic act.

Now, you may find this too cloying or too pretentious. Maybe. It really depends on the *context*. Perhaps the speaker desires a bit of fun. An outrageous bit of fun that drags the listener out of daily habitual boredom and into the realm of fantastical life. The speaker is saying to the listener: "Alright, I know this might be out of the ordinary, but let's entertain this zany notion about words, let's dance this exuberant dance, life is short, the world is wondrous, our ability to describe such a world is infinite and uninhibited and I am going to use language to wake both of us up a bit. Do you wanna play?"

This is the playfulness of **Auxesis** (Ox EE sis): *the use of an extraordinary or heightened word in place of an ordinary, habitual word*. The Greek origin of this word literally means "increase" or "amplification." By finding an extraordinary word to replace a humdrum word, you are powering that word, making it more "important." You are amplifying that subject, revving its motor. From the early Greeks onward, schoolkids learned to appreciate the heightened appeal of language and would practice describing a commonplace object by shining an extrastrength verbal spotlight on it.

Today's actors are often told that words, especially pompous ones, are artificial, so they miss out on the kind of verbal practice that allowed performers of more daring centuries to exploit the theatricality of language. By practicing extraordinary words or phrases, the schoolkids of classical antiquity were working with humor, with wit, and were becoming adept at "reinventing" the world.

William Shakespeare's comedy *Love's Labour's Lost* parodies the elaborate verbal training he received in the Elizabethan schoolroom. The play's characters (particularly Holofernes, the pedantic schoolmaster!) are always searching for the extraordinary verbal expression. They shun ordinariness, reaching instead for that Promethean flame at every opportunity. Their world is one where auxesis is the preferred "norm." It is sometimes subtle and sometimes

Chapter Two

extreme. For the pompous extremities, note the following exchange between Holofernes the Schoolmaster and Armado the Fantastical Spaniard, who are sparring, showing off their verbal hipness.

> ARMADO: Sir, it is the king's most sweet pleasure and affection to congratulate the princess at her pavilion in the posteriors of the day, which the rude multitude call the afternoon.
>
> HOLOFERNES: The posterior of the day, most generous sir, is liable, congruent, and measurable for the afternoon: the word is well culled, chosen, sweet and apt, I do assure you, sir, I do assure.
>
> (5.1)

Armado's rechristening of "afternoon" as the "posteriors of the day" meets with the critical approval of Holofernes, who—not to be outdone—notes that the posterior of the day is "liable, congruent, and measurable for the afternoon." In his reply, the lofty "liable" and "congruent" stand for *suitable*, while the clinical "measurable" stands for *appropriate*. Translation: "Your phrase is a suitable, appropriate one for the afternoon." The verbal radar is set at maximum sensitivity in this play. It trains us, the listener, to be on the alert for outlandish verbiage. Shakespeare both pokes fun at—and celebrates—this outlandishness. Only someone trained in Elizabethan grammar schools could capture this exuberant verbal spirit and make it part of the play's subject.

What does an actor make of this kind of language? How to play this kind of part today? The first step is *awareness*. One must increase one's awareness that the language is brimming "over the top." If you are not aware that the words are "extraordinary," you may be likely to walk right by them. Wit and humor are the casualties of such unawareness. If you are not aware that the words are super spicy, you may "speak right through them" as if you were ordering a burger and fries. But these words are not ordinary morsels. Auxesis requires the actor to bite into succulent words, to roll them around the palate, to taste the words as if one is eating especially exotic food. All wrapped in a serving of sheer delight:

POWERING THE TEXT: Amplification

✔ Taste the Words; that is, bite into them

Four centuries after the verbal pomp and parody of *Love's Labour's Lost*, Tony Kushner introduced us to The Homebody, who gloriously—even if rather apologetically—inherits the spirit of auxesis in his fascinating play *Homebody/Kabul*. The Homebody, a quirky British woman with an extraordinary passion for the exotica and magic of bygone historical eras, particularly in remote corners of the ancient world, opens the play with a tour de force one-hour monologue or "lecture" on the history of Afghanistan. Except it's not really a lecture. It's partly a travelogue and historical narrative that is continually interrupted by The Homebody's eccentric personal ruminations and reflections. Like a train that constantly jumps its tracks, The Homebody goes off on wildly bewitching and humorous personal tangents. Exotic and extraordinary language is part of her story. She is intoxicated with the world and the fabulous verbal means to capture it. Her vision of the world is so outrageous and delightful that she requires equally outrageous and delightful words to describe it.

So she builds her entire story, in large part, on the platform of auxesis.

"I love love love love the world!" exclaims The Homebody. She follows this outpouring with a self-effacing critique, in which she presumes that we, the audience, have come to view her as a simpleton. She then offers an almost pitiable sort of defense.

> I cannot hope to *contravene* your *peremptory low estimation*, which may for all its *peremptoriness* nevertheless be exactly appropriate. I live with the world's mild censure, or would do were it the case that I ever strayed far enough from my modesty, or should I say my essential *surfeit of inconsequence*, to so far attract the world's attention as to provoke from it its mild censure.
>
> (Act 1, italics mine)

Look at the lofty flight of her amplified words and phrases. She does not oppose or dispute, she *contravenes*. She does not say "lousy opinion," she prefers the elaborate arc of *peremptory low estimation*. Others may opt for "modesty," but The Homebody ultimately prefers the extravagance of *surfeit of inconsequence*. The Homebody coaches us, really, trains our ear to be vigilant

Chapter Two

in listening, in picking up the verbal clues scattered among this beautifully strange monologue. The actor playing this part has to give these heightened words special emphasis, wrap them in enthusiastic colors. Again, taste them, bite into their excess.

To further increase our verbal consciousness, The Homebody openly calls attention to her language. "So my diction, my syntax, well, it's so *irritating*, I apologize, I do, it's very hard." And for good measure, she adds, "My parents don't speak like this; no one I know does; no one does." But she can't help herself. Throughout her long and winding piece, she prays regularly to her God, Auxesis. Instead of saying, "thin, Jewish prayer caps," she opts for the staggeringly mysterious, "attenuated yarmulkite millanarisms." Millanarisms, she quickly tells us, are hats. Later she confides to us that she keeps a library of "antilegomenoi"—castoff or forgotten pieces of knowledge.

This role begs for an actor who will step up and unapologetically *defend* the language. It requires an actor who is willing to burst out of the conservative straits of naturalistic dialogue and its very safe, very predictable vocal strategy. Auxesis dares the performer to have a twinkle in the eye, a brashness of expression.

Cool American Lingo

Let's cross the Atlantic and cruise into the urban American landscape of the 20th century to view different aspects of the Promethean flame, to see how this light burns on the gritty and jazzy streets of Americana. In Eric Overmyer's *In a Pig's Valise*, a sendup and celebration of 1940s Raymond Chandler American detective novels and films, our hard-boiled hero, James Taxi, in front of the Heartbreak Hotel at the corner of Neon and Lonely, is giving us a cool Philip Marlowe–like introduction to his story:

> It was two-fifty-two in the fretful A.M. I'd been ensconced in the back of my Chevy Bel-Air....I found myself shivering in my shoes—scratch that—my gumshoes, on one of the worst corners in this quadrant of Western Civ. There were a lot of corners reserved for the criminally insane in this behind-the-eight-ball burg, but this one was special. Neon and Lonely.

POWERING THE TEXT: Amplification

Taxi drags on his cigarette and continues:

> I'd come in from the valley. Forty-suck-your-heart-out miles of fast food and singed ozone. Avec shot brakes and smoldering upholstery. I was risking a loitering rap in front of a beanbag hotel. The kind of dive where checkout time sometimes comes when you least expect it. Loitering with intent: to meet some mysterioso-ette. Here. In the shadow of The Heartbreak.
>
> (Act 1)

This is good stuff. Overmyer is a playwright who celebrates rich and colorful American slang and the jazz of American idioms that reveal the "extraordinary" in our speaking. A parody of classic 1940s detective lingo, a heightened talk, is part of this self-conscious sendup of the "Black-and-White" American Private Eye genre. Look at this parade of sizzling one-liners:

fretful A.M.
ensconced in the back of my Chevy Bel-Air
shoes—scratch that—gumshoes
quadrant of Western Civ
behind-the-eight-ball burg
Forty-suck-your-heart-out miles of fast food and singed ozone
Avec shot brakes and smoldering upholstery
dive
mysterioso-ette

The less intrepid among us are up at two fifty-two in the *morning*; we are *seated*, not "ensconced," in a Chevy Bel-Air; we are in a particular *section of town*, not in a "quadrant of Western Civ" or a "behind-the-eight-ball burg." Most of us would say "*with* shot brakes" rather than the French, "*avec* shot brakes." We leave the smog and boredom of the valley, as compared to the "forty-suck-your-heart-out miles of fast food and singed ozone." Not James Taxi. His lingo is part of his being.

Chapter Two

> **When a character needs the extravagance of language to match his extravagance of living he often takes a shot of Auxesis—straight up.**

Taxi's larger-than-life lingo complements his larger-than-life persona. That's why auxesis is an actor's character-building tool. It provides clues about behavior. For Taxi, nothing is taken for granted. Not even the concept of hotel "checkout time," which he turns into a clever pun. And, finally, Taxi is curious to meet some "mysterioso-ette," a sultry-voiced *woman* who has called him and arranged for a rendezvous at the Heartbreak.

The actor can really "point up" this dialogue, especially the phrases of cool auxesis. They are meant to be enjoyed, "served up" to the audience like a decadent piece of dessert. Bite into the consonants, savor the phrases. Another way for the performer to get a handle on auxesis is to imagine a specific context for this language: The actor is saying to the audience, "Check out this phrase," "Are we having fun?" "We are going into a world of smoky clubs, suspicious characters, tantalizing clues, blinking neon lights, fedoras slouched low, ruby-red lipstick on a cocktail glass, romantic escapades—are you with me? Isn't it neat that we have such a genre?"

Turn on your radar. In any play where the language informs the story, your antennas become fine-tuned, ready to capture any elevated verbal signal that enters into your listening. Instead of talking to himself, Taxi notes that he is "cogitating a capella." He puffs on a "coffin nail," and, in an effort to test the truthfulness of a witness, Taxi will "check her pulse" or "scan her polygraph."

Listen to this passage. Taxi doesn't have a secretary; he has a faithful "amanuensis." Taxi never walks; he "saunters." He never sleeps; he "grabs some shut-eye." Why go to a bar when you can hang out at the local "gin joint"?

> After I hung up the horn, I closed the office for the afternoon. I gave my faithful amanuensis, "Legs" Lichtenstein, the rest of the week off. She'd earned it. I hadn't paid her since fiscal '57. Legs. What a word jockey. But that's another story. I sauntered over to my local gin joint and tossed down a couple of muscles. For you rookies out there, a muscle is a standard-issue detective drink: Kahlua and Maalox. Then I grabbed some shut-eye in the back of my Chevy.
>
> (Act 1)

POWERING THE TEXT: Amplification

Many contemporary actors are often embarrassed by "verbal excess," finding it uncomfortable to dig into this kind of dialogue. And so they shy away from it. Well, yes, there is a danger of becoming so obsessed with the verbal fireworks that we lose sight of the character, the objectives, the relationship with the scene partner, the play. We become talking machines. That is always a danger. But verbally adventurous dialogue cannot detonate if we don't light the fuse. It needs our bravest impulses and our most playful selves. Taxi and his client, the mysterioso-ette, Dolores Con Leche, are keenly attuned to each other's words, always ready to play.

> TAXI: I like a gal who can spin a phrase.
> DOLORES: I like a guy who can torture all day a figure of speech.
> TAXI: Not to mention syntax.
> (Act 2)

How can we fully understand the roles if we shortchange the full vocal expression of that character, especially since the language is providing such important hints? We can always pull back if we decide we've gone too far in our exploration. But the exploration itself is necessary. Let us choose to explore.

Auxesis shakes up the world, rearranges it, often for humorous or wondrous effect. This bold figure escorts us to another universe, where words celebrate our aliveness and our ability to imagine a new way to describe some portion of our experience.

Look at Juliet in her unbridled excitement in waiting for Romeo to come to her balcony to consummate their relationship. She knows he is coming under the cover of night, but streaks of daylight are still visible. Juliet implores the night to arrive with all speed in these memorable lines that almost bounce off the page.

> Gallop apace you fiery footed steeds
> Toward Phoebus' lodging, such a waggoner
> As Phaeton would whip you to the west
> And bring in cloudy night immediately.
> (3.2)

Chapter Two

Unlike James Taxi and The Homebody, Juliet plays the heightened language "straight." She does not admit to its extravagance, she takes it at face value. She does not editorialize about style; she simply exploits the mythological allusions. Elizabethans knew that Phoebus was the sun god whose chariot was pulled daily across the sky by horses. They knew about his reckless son, Phaeton, who, in driving the chariot one day, went too fast and lost control, dropping the chariot perilously close to the earth, scorching the grounds. For Juliet, on this night, she desires the speeding Phaeton to be the chariot's driver, so that the sun could be pulled across the sky with racecar haste. Night is her accomplice.

For Juliet, nothing less than this image and this kind of language will suffice. Language ignites character. Her being is large, her longing mythical in scale, and her communication literally reaches for the heavens through this amplificatory figure of auxesis.

To express her fully, the performer, like Juliet, needs maximum horsepower, all the gears of her industrial chariot.

DIAZEUGMA
The Propelling Figure

A lonely Soviet bureaucrat, swigging vodka with a young woman, describes the miraculous workings of the Soviet Communist Party.

> The Party drove away the Czar, immortalized Lenin, withstood France and Britain and the United States, made Communism in one country, electrified Russia, milled steel, built railways, abolished distance, defeated Germany, suspended time, became Eternal, dispersed the body of each and every member, molecule by molecule, across an inconceivably vast starry matrix encompassing the infinite.
>
> (2.1)

In the above passage from Tony Kushner's *Slavs!*, the Soviet Party takes many separate actions, indicated by the verbs. The actions or verbs are strung together,

POWERING THE TEXT: Amplification

like a string of pearls, and they are all connected to a single subject—the Party. The Party is the string that holds all of the pearls:

the Party:
drove away
immortalized
withstood
made
electrified
milled
built
abolished
defeated
suspended
became
dispersed

One subject, twelve verbs. **Diazeugma** (die ah ZOOG ma) *occurs when one subject feeds many verbs, creating a heightened sequence of action.* The effect of such a strategy is to make action more suspenseful, keeping the audience in a state of uncertainty as to the final outcome. It amplifies action while throwing interest forward in the sentence. Zeugma, in early Greek, means a "yoking" while diazeugma implies the opposite, a "disjoining." A disjoining in the sense that the majority of the verbs are separated—or disjoined—from the subject by a considerable distance.

Let's see how actors can take advantage of this propelling figure. Diazeugma appears in a variety of moods and forms across a wide range of plays. Sometimes it appears overtly and sometimes covertly. Its covert—and hysterical—usage can be found in Congreve's Restoration gem, *The Way of the World*. In this bustling world of social gossip, scheming, witty repartee, too much rouge, fabulous wigs, two pretentious dandies, Witwoud and Fainall, are forever on the romantic prowl, hoping—in their foppish outlandishness—to capture the eyes and ears of the ladies. At a London chocolate house (the Starbucks of London's early 18th century), Witwoud describes the eccentricities of his friend Sir Fainall, who has discovered an ingenious way to increase his social status and heighten his self-importance.

Chapter Two

> Why he would slip you out of this chocolate house, just when you had been talking to him—(*As soon as your back was turned—whip he was gone*)—then trip to his lodging, clap on a hood and scarf and a mask, slap into a hackney coach, and drive hither to the door again in a trice; where he would send in for himself, that I mean, call for himself, wait for himself, nay and what's more, not finding himself, sometimes leave a letter for himself.
>
> (1.8)

It seems that Fainall would run home, disguise himself, call a cab, return to the chocolate shop, ask for himself, and—not finding himself—leave a letter for himself! Witwoud's speech has delicious buoyancy that is propelled by the action of diazeugma. One subject, "he," propels a slew of verbs:

he:
    would [a helping verb]
        slip [you] out
        trip to
        clap on
        slap into
        drive

Then, lest we should forget, Witwoud repeats the subject again:

he:
    would
        send in
        call for
        wait for
        leave a letter

Besides highlighting the subject, the actor must give a little extra **stress** or **accent** to the verbs so that the sentence can keep hurtling forward—and so that we are reminded of its connection to the subject—*he*. Each verb "pushes" or "jolts" the sentence forward. [Note: the verb, "slip you out" is an 18th-century expression for "slip out."] Think again of our car analogy. Each verb is a separate gear shift, with each increasing gear pushing the speech to a

POWERING THE TEXT: Amplification

final destination—"leave a letter for himself." This car has nine main gears. But stressing verbs is not enough. Stress must work together with a sustained *inflection* that tells the audience that there is more to come—wait➔hang on➔look at this!➔can you believe this?! As a result, the actor must avoid down-endings in this speech because the sprint is not over until we get to the end.

Remember that this speech consists of only *one* sentence. The verbs sustain the speech by continually describing a different *action* and creating a kind of suspense. What will be the outcome? This does not mean that the surrounding words are unimportant—far from it—but it does suggest that the forward progress of diazeugma is fueled by the action words. The performer cannot linger or downglide along the route of this speech.

> Why ↓ he would…slip you out ↓ of this chocolate house, just when you had been talking to him ↓ —(As soon as your back was turned—whip he was gone)…then trip ↓ to his lodging, clap ↓ on a hood…and scarf, and a mask…slap ↓ into a hackney coach, and drive hither to the door again…in a trice.

The sentence is not meditative; it is frolicking and rhythmic and active. Like big band jazz, it swings. It takes you by the hand and says, "Let's go; jump aboard."

For a more overt—and ominous—usage of the Propelling Figure we can examine a servant-gentlewoman's description of an increasingly paranoiac Lady Macbeth, who has begun to walk the castle battlements late at night. Speaking to a doctor, the gentlewoman describes strange behavior, the eerie sleepwalking of a disturbed Lady Macbeth.

> I have seen her rise from the bed, throw her night-gown upon her, unlock her closet, take forth paper, fold it, write upon it, read it, afterwards seal it, and again return to bed; yet all this while in a most fast sleep.
>
> (5.1)

In a somewhat altered grammatical construction, the verbs are connected to the direct object, "her":

Chapter Two

I have seen **her**
> *rise*
> *throw*
> *unlock*
> *take forth*
> *fold*
> *write upon*
> *read*
> *seal*
> *return*

Here the verbs propel a kind of ritualistic rhythm that mirrors Lady Macbeth's ritualized behavior. The line has a sparse almost mechanized rhythm that is aided by the verbal craft of *asyndeton*, the deliberate omission of conjunctions (e.g., "and," "but"). Stripped of any connecting tissue, the sharp procession of verbs provides a staccato rhythm that the actor can play. By giving each verb an accent, the actor exploits the stark ritualized or mechanical actions of a compulsive Lady Macbeth. Each verb spurs a little more fascination, a little more suspense, as her action comes full circle, ending where it started—back in bed, "fast asleep."

Verbs carry action. A barrage of verbs carries amplified action, especially when connected to a single subject. That is the strategy of diazeugma, which seeks to involve us in a blow-by-blow account of a heightened sequence. This Propelling Figure wants us to stay tuned, to stay awake, to "follow the money." It is one more amplifying tool that the performer can use in persuading an audience.

TAKING STOCK

Figures of amplification are propulsive figures. They are full of vigor and aliveness. They always want more out of life, that extra edge. These restless figures are not satisfied with polite conversation. They generate a torrent of sounds and rhythms and vocal detonations. They accumulate, rename, get outrageous, look for action. They are suspicious of the casual and the mellow.

POWERING THE TEXT: Amplification

Today's Laid-Back Nonconfrontational Lukewarm Persona stands at odds with the performance demands of amplification. Low exertion and low "speaking" are the results of such a persona. This casual low-gear speaking pervades large swaths of our contemporary culture.

Watch a scene from one of the many crime or detective shows on television. More than likely, the scene is filled with moody pauses, broken bits of dialogue, sighs, and glances, with characters often struggling to express themselves. This is the contemporary *style*. It casts a huge shadow over today's actors. It discourages actors from the use of amplifying verbal power. It views such adventure as extreme and nonrealistic. However, today's dialogue and acting is not any closer to "reality" than the quick, snappy, witty repartee of a 1940s Cary Grant or Bette Davis movie. If you have not watched one of these movies for a while, you may be amazed as to the amount of crisp, accumulating dialogue per minute of screen time. Compare it to a contemporary minute of screen time. Do you hear a difference? Behavior tends to dominate a scene today, while language tended to dominate in those earlier decades. They are different approaches, different styles.

Let's go. You have your main gears—accumulatio, appositio, auxesis, and diazeugma. They are imported parts with an American attitude. Now, jump into that hotrod car, buckle up. The horses are waiting to take you on a journey. Ignite the power and delight that this vehicle, *Amplification*, offers to the bold, dynamic performer.

Chapter Three

SPEAKING IN CLOSE-UPS:
Image & Description

The image. Our dazzling world of electronic media floods our daily lives with a rapid succession of digital images. The great Techno God, *Image*, offers us a stunning visual palette from which we can select our favors: we Snapchat, we Instagram, we pin pictures on Pinterest boards, we post selfies and the latest vacation photo on Facebook. With a touch of our iPhones, we send wedding pictures across the world in mere seconds. Films sweep us into a sea of computer-enhanced images, while laptops bombard us with livestreams and alluring icons. Towering skyscrapers function as massive digital billboards, flashing bold graphics, pop superstars, glitzy ads, and all things titillating in an endless parade of outsized eye candy.

These are the wonders of our contemporary techno-savvy world. We marvel, quite understandably, at what technology hath wrought. Of the previous 100,000 years of human history, we stand today in the privileged Digital Midas Zone, where every swipe of our finger miraculously produces an image. So we bow before the great Techno God, Image, and cannot imagine a life without its digital blessings. We are hooked. We are addicted. And yet every great leap forward carries with it a sacrifice. For every innovation we often pay a price. We frequently are not cognizant of the costs exacted for our newfound electronic paradise. Today, we know, even if we take it for granted, what we have gained. But do we know what we have lost?

What happens to our ability to communicate when techno gadgetry shoulders most of the responsibility for image and description? If *electronica* creates so much of the image today, what effect does this have on the contemporary actor and her ability to communicate? What, if anything, has she lost? How has electronic entertainment altered what we expect of the performer? If the world were to suddenly unplug itself, who would be capable of conjuring the image?

SPEAKING IN CLOSE-UPS: Image & Description

To find the answer to these questions, we must step outside the bedazzling box of our digital times and look for perspective across earlier centuries. The closer we look, the more fascinating the discoveries.

Without the benefit of iPhones, apps, boom mikes, DSLR cameras, editing rooms, tape loops, computer animation, and special effects, the pre-21st-century performer had to rely on something else in describing an event. The performer had to rely on the Human Speaking Voice, the Word, and the enormous resources of Imagination, Craft, and Courage in telling a story. This was not an ordinary use of the human voice, not an ordinary use of the Word, certainly not an ordinary display of imagination, craft, or courage. The bar was set at Olympian heights that required the performer to "reach higher" than any height known to us today. Think stratospheric.

This expectation created performance muscles that we rarely flex today (because we are not called upon to do so), and it inspired actors to exert and extend themselves in order to produce the necessary results required by the *listening* audience. The "reaching" for an image, the amount of intense training required to deliver lines of graphic description, was striking in its commitment and execution. This was one of the great performance secrets of classical antiquity, one that wound its way to Shakespeare and beyond.

Sitting at the center of this secret was the firm conviction that spoken words can evoke powerful visual phenomena in the mind's eye of the listener.

We know from historical records that schoolkids of classical antiquity received formal training in description and image. Poet-bards and epic singers had been developing this idea for centuries, but the actual introduction of teaching techniques would start in the 5th century B.C. The early Greeks created entire categories of description, each capturing a distinct chunk of the physical universe: description of the earth (geographia); description of water (hydrographia); description of a person and body (characterismus); and description of an action or event (pragmatographia) are a few specific examples of this fascination with describing the world through words. All of these specific categories were subsumed under a major rubric, *Enargia* (en AR gee a), which was concerned with evoking visual phenomena through language.

Chapter Three

So in this chapter we will focus on **Enargia**, the Mother of Image and Description, to gain a clearer view of how human—as opposed to digital—power evoked visual stimuli and stoked the fire of human storytelling. We will also take a glance at how the subsidiary figure of **Onomatopoeia** helped charge the power of Enargia.

ENARGIA
Cinema of Words

The pre-electronic world was utterly fascinated with depicting the actions of human beings and all things across the cosmos. They could either talk about it or they could paint it. There was nothing to plug in. For the talker, words and human imagination would be the chariot carrying the orator and his audience across the colorful terrain of visual phenomena. In early rhetorical training, the great umbrella term of description and visual phenomena was **Enargia**—which emphasized the *speaker's ability to evoke visually powerful description and to portray it with such graphic immediacy that the listener felt that he was, in effect, seeing the described event "before his eyes."*

To be able to bring an image "before your eyes," as Aristotle noted, was a very high calling and responsibility. It separated the great speakers from the merely good speakers. The American scholar and theorist Richard Lanham has noted that the rockstar orator, Lysias, was praised for making his listener feel that he could "see" the described actions and for making him sense that he is meeting "face-to-face" the various characters of the story. Enargia, then, is not a pattern (like antithesis) or a run (like accumulatio). It is not a particular verbal formula. It is a *commitment*. It is a *context*, an *expectation* about the ability of the performer to evoke visual cues.

Enargia is a moment-to-moment cinema of speaking.

To understand the mechanism of this descriptive immediacy, we can start by looking at the early Greek roots of Enargia—"vividness" and "distinctness." **Vividness. Distinctness.** Make a poster of these two words and hang them on your wall. These words ring out as the antidote to vague generality.

SPEAKING IN CLOSE-UPS: Image & Description

Only when an actor develops an extraordinary appreciation for what it means for something to be distinct, for what it means to achieve vividness, can she begin to attain that "before your eyes" visual immediacy that makes an audience sit still, stop chewing gum or looking at the wristwatch, forget about dinner plans after the show, the babysitter, tomorrow's office meeting, 1,001 tasks not related to the play. Enargia is concerned with a riveting experience, a be-here-now, watch-this-heart-stopping-detail kind of experience. Enargia says to an audience: "Look at this incredible footage."

What does it take to activate the cinema of words? How does an actor achieve vivid and distinct verbal footage in performance? The clues can be found in a very old story. Over 2,700 years ago, the cinema of Homer's *Iliad* hit the Mediterranean world—and, in many ways, it established a way of performing and a way of telling a story that has lasted to the present day. With its unforgettable accounts of the battles at Troy, the portrayals of great mythic characters like Achilles, Hector, and Agamemnon, its themes of loss and betrayal, and its depiction of the fall of the House of Priam—the *Iliad* laid the foundation for our Western narrative and helped shape our modern identity.

This epic story, bound in twenty-four "books," contains 15,690 lines of heroic Greek verse, over half of which are in the form of descriptive narrative. The remaining lines are in the form of direct speech, where a character, like Hector, addresses another character. While some form of rudimentary writing may have been available to Homer, many scholars now believe that much of the work was composed orally and that the poetic stanzas were specifically composed for oral delivery. That is, the writer spoke it into being, composed it out loud (and perhaps wrote it down), and memorized its progress across thousands of lines.

How was this possible? The short answer is that the work was conceived as a performance, as an occasion for speaking ("acting") before an audience. As such, the author "performed" the lines in the act of composition, instilling a powerful connection between words and memory. Striking and distinct visual cues abound, as in this riveting description of Agamemnon's warsuit.

> Agamemnon boomed out a command
> For his men to arm, and did so himself,
> Strapping on sunlit bronze, his *greaves* first,   [*shin armor*]

Chapter Three

> Works of art, trimmed with silver at the ankles.
> Then he covered his chest with a *corselet*...   [*breastplate*]
> It had ten bands of dark blue enamel,
> Twelve of gold, and twenty of tin.
> On either side were three enameled dragons
> With arching necks—iridescent as rainbows
> That Zeus anchors in cloud as portents for men.
> And he slung a sword around his shoulders,
> Golden bolts shining in the hilt. The sheath
> Was silver, fitted with golden straps.
> Then he took up his shield, a crafted glory
> Of metalwork, ringed with bronze, *bossed*   [*studded*]
> With white tin, and inlaid with dark *cyan*,   [*greenish-blue*]
> A Gorgon flanked by Terror and Rout
> Glaring out of the midnight blue center.
> The shield was hung with a *baldric* of silver   [*belt*]
> Upon which writhed an enameled dragon
> With three heads twisting from a single neck.
> He set upon his head a two-horned helmet
> With four bosses and a horsehair plume
> That nodded menacingly on its crest.
>
> (Book 11, lines 15–41, trans. by Stanley Lombardo, italics mine)

It's a feast of images. Ironically—and remarkably—this ancient text seems ideally suited to our contemporary language of filmmaking. Let's try it. The speaker's "camera" zooms in on each part of the warsuit, focusing on graphic detail, panning slowly up from the legs to the chest to the head. Along the way the camera zooms in on Agamemnon's sword, shield, and helmet. Vividness. Distinctness. Can you follow this footage?

The narrator is speaking in close-ups.

It is not a long shot where everything blurs into sameness. It is a series of *close-ups*. No detail escapes the searching eye of the narrator as he pans across the mighty warrior:

SPEAKING IN CLOSE-UPS: Image & Description

LEGS
    strapping on **greaves**
    trimmed with silver at the **ankles**

BREASTPLATE
    ten bands of dark blue enamel
    spaced by **twelve bands** of gold and twenty of tin
    six enameled serpents arch their necks
    three on each side, shimmering bright as rainbows

AROUND HIS SHOULDERS
    he slung a **sword**
    golden **bolts** shining at hilt
    the **sheath** is silver
    fitted with golden **straps**

SHIELD
    with **rings of bronze**
    studded with white tin
    Gorgon stares from the blue center
    flanked by **Terror** and **Rout**

SHIELD BELT
    in silver
    with a writhing enameled **dragon** running along it
    with **three heads twisting from a single neck**

UPON HIS HEAD
    is set a **helmet**
    fronted with **four studs** and forked with **two horns**
    and a horsehair **plume**

This breakdown provides guides for how an actor may speak in close-ups. The author has *composed* a series of close-ups, but it is the actor who must now *speak* and *realize* these magnified images.

Chapter Three

Owning the Words

To speak in close-ups, an extraordinary commitment to each image is required. It is not enough to intellectually understand an image. The actor must completely *own* each image, paint it in his mind's eye, so as to vividly present it to a listener. If you have never seen greaves or "shin armor" before, you must go and find it. Either online, in books, or in life. Pick it up. Feel it. Look at it—carefully. You cannot speak "shin armor" in close-up if you have never seen it. Your speaking will be vague and general rather than vivid and distinct.

What do the six serpents on Agamemnon's breastplate look like? Draw them. That will brand the image into your body and mind. If you have no familiarity with serpents, go online or to medieval art books and find some. Gaze at them. Zoom in on a serpent. Emblazon its image in your mind's eye. Can you draw one now? Or can you describe it to a friend?

You cannot deliver an image to an audience that you do not *own*.

A very specific 100 percent realization of that image is paramount. Can you see it clearly before you in your imagination? If not, keep looking at the serpent. Eventually you will feel confident that you own the image of a serpent. At that point you are ready to make that image appear "before our eyes."

Nothing less than full descriptive *ownership* will activate energia, the art of speaking in close-ups. Each line of this speech requires enormous commitment to image, a moment-to-moment, frame-by-frame immediacy. What does Agamemnon's breastplate, with its bands of blue enamel, gold, and tin, look like? Do you have a vivid picture of the dragon rippling along Agamemnon's shield belt with its three twisting heads? How about the subtle details, like the golden bolts on the hilt of his sword? Take nothing for granted.

You may also need to do a bit of research, not for scholarly purposes, but for access to image ownership. A Gorgon's face appears in the heart of Agamemnon's shield, against a background of bulging blue metal. What's a Gorgon? When you discover that a Gorgon is any of the three mythological sisters with snakes for hair, whose terrifying gaze turned men to stone—you have a starting point for energia.

SPEAKING IN CLOSE-UPS: Image & Description

Now you need to find a specific image for a Gorgon. Hit the art books again (unless there is a Gorgon walking in your neighborhood), search for an image that resonates with you. It is only after you have branded the image in your mind's eye that you can deliver it—in full Technicolor—to an audience, who will be hearing and seeing it for the first time.

What about the twin gods of Terror and Rout, who flank the Gorgon? Who are they and what do they look like? You may discover that Terror was sometimes depicted with a lion's head. Can this discovery bring graphic immediacy to your speaking?

The Actor as Editor

The *Iliad*, along with its companion story, the *Odyssey*, served as the enargia-in-training for generations of young performers and speakers during the golden age of Hellenic Greek civilization—and for centuries beyond. Schoolkids cut their teeth on its stunning descriptive sequences, as they practiced owning the images. Every week, young performers would memorize and deliver excerpts from this epic story in seeking to make their classroom audience "see" the sword-flashing battles and "hear" the emotionally charged speeches of its principal players.

This kind of training makes the human performer responsible for evoking visual phenomena. Students learned to re-create the scenes of this sweeping saga and, after a period of apprenticeship, were ready to tackle the major technical challenge of ***pragmatographia***—descriptions of ***action***, as in the following vivid portrayal of Achilles' defilement of the corpse of Hector, the great Trojan warrior and archenemy of the Greeks.

> But it was shame and defilement Achilles
> Had in mind for Hector. He pierced the tendons
> Above the heels and cinched them with leather thongs
> To his chariot, letting Hector's head drag.
> He mounted, hoisted up the prize armor,
> And whipped his team to a willing gallop
> Across the plain. A cloud of dust rose

Chapter Three

> Where Hector was hauled, and the long black hair
> Fanned out from his head, so beautiful once,
> As it trailed in the dust.
>
> (Book 22, lines 438–448, trans. by Stanley Lombardo)

Look at the level of graphic detail in this sequence. Again, look at how this old text seems to prefigure the modern camera's use of perspective. Some camera "shots" are super close-ups, others from a distance, while others are traveling shots. How does the speaker show each shot or image to a listening audience, and how does he make it distinct? What separates one image from another?

Editing

Not the electronic kind, but the human kind. Watch a film today. How does the director guide you across a field of images? She sits in an editing room with an editor and electronically arranges a visual sequence that captivates you. Every time the screen or frame changes, you experience the art of editing.

Zoom in on pierced tendons, pull back to reveal feet being fastened to back of chariot, pan across body to Hector's head dragging behind, a close-up of Achilles mounting the chariot, a traveling shot of horses being whipped into a gallop, a long traveling shot of dust rising from the body, a super close-up of Hector's long black hair fanning out in the dust, a final long shot of a chariot racing across the plain. The images bounce around, darting in and out, stoking our fascination. Each image is distinct. Editing controls our ability to follow the story; it controls our emotional response, depending on how the sequence is spliced together.

Human beings have the same ability to edit a visual sequence through their voice and communicative power.

To understand how *vocal* editing works, we can simply note, for a start, each change of frame as we listen to the descriptive sequence of Achilles' debasing of Hector's body. Every time the screen changes, we want to note it:

SPEAKING IN CLOSE-UPS: Image & Description

Achilles PIERCES TENDONS above the heels

LASHES heels and feet to chariot with leather thongs

Hector's HEAD DRAGS on ground

Achilles MOUNTS chariot

HOISTS UP dead man's armor   [*war booty*]

WHIPS chariot horses into a GALLOP

CLOUD OF DUST rises from Hector's BODY

Hector's LONG BLACK HAIR FANS OUT in dust

Hair and chariot moving across the plain

There are distinct "shots" in this sequence. There are distinct changes of frame. The actor needs to "edit" this sequence for an audience to follow the specific changes occurring on the screen.

Each new shot requires a separate vocal tone or stress.

The voice changes because the need changes: The actor *needs* that new image, wants the audience to *see* it, so he uses his voice to "point up" a new image on the screen. It is the vocal equivalent of a movie screen changing from one shot to another. The actor, in effect, is saying: "Look at this! Don't miss this next detail. Now here comes a different arresting image. Wait—look at this new detail that has just entered the frame. Can you see the hair fanning out in the dust as the chariot races across the plain?"

When you have a burning desire to present each distinct image, your voice will find the shades of tone and stress and intensity to edit the story for your listener. When something is important to you, when you have an extraordinary urge to re-create an event, you find the vocal editing impulses that demand extraordinary listening. Speaking and listening: the two sides work together.

> **Energia encourages the actor to edit a visual sequence, to make blazing vocal distinctions between one image and another, so that the "screen" changes before our eyes.**

Chapter Three

But too many actors tend to speak descriptive sequences like Achilles' defilement of Hector's body as one generalized blast. One long shot of sameness. There is no editing of the text for an audience. Imagine watching a movie in which there were no close-ups, no zoom-ins, no traveling shots, very few changes of frame, where everything was presented in the blurry distance, a long shot, one image almost identical with the next. It would be a long night at the movies, a frustrating exercise in self-control. The film would not sustain interest or the audience's participation in the story. And yet many audiences attending live theater face this same dilemma. They don't feel connected to the story or to a descriptive speech that seeks to convey the clash and spark of exciting action. They get frustrated, feel the language is beyond them, and tune out.

Visual distinctness and vividness are a challenge for all who tread the boards of the stage—including for one intrepid actor-turned-writer, Will Shakespeare.

Shakespeare in the Editing Room

Born during a time when the Word was ablaze, a time of cultural rejuvenation and discovery, Shakespeare met his age and pushed it forward. Trained to unleash verbal imagery in the classroom, Shakespeare, like generations of British students before him, learned to recite the visually stirring stanzas of Ovid's *Metamorphosis*, Virgil's *Aeneid*, and other Latin classics. These Latin works featured the descriptive hallmark of enargia. Later, as a man of the theater, as an actor, and finally as an emerging playwright, Shakespeare was thoroughly intrigued with how words work on an audience. He knew that spoken words could spur the visual imagination of his audience and hold them spellbound. He realized that actors could take an audience across the ocean and back again, as the play changes "scenery" and travels vast distances in the span of two hours at the Globe Theatre. He experiments and, at times, deliberately toys with this concept.

In his *Henry V*, Shakespeare creates the role of the Chorus, whose job is to paint descriptive transitions and re-create graphic visual cues for the audience. Enargia. It's a deliberately self-conscious, playful strategy. The Chorus

SPEAKING IN CLOSE-UPS: Image & Description

is the imaginative canvas onto which the audience can "see" changes in location and a parade of exciting events. As King Henry and his naval fleet embark for battles in France, the Chorus provides this compelling "live coverage" of the ships shoving off from shore.

> Suppose that you have seen
> The well-appointed king at Hampton Pier
> Embark his royalty—and his brave fleet
> With silken streamers the young *Phoebus fanning*.   [*fluttering against morning sun*]
> Play with your fancies!—and in them behold
> Upon the hempen tackle ship-boys climbing;
> Hear the shrill whistle which doth order give
> To sounds confused. Behold the threaden sails,
> Borne with the invisible and creeping wind,
> Draw the huge *bottoms* through the furrowed sea,   [*ships*]
> Breasting the lofty surge. O, do but think
> You stand upon the *rivage* and behold   [*shore*]
> A city on the inconstant billows dancing,
> For so appears this fleet majestical,
> Holding due course for Harfleur.
>
> (3.1, italics mine)

"Play with your fancies!" the Chorus implores us. That's what enargia required, the active participation of the audience, which, together with the actor, could re-create a fleet of ships floating on the sea. Look how the Chorus edits this colorful event. To provide a more vivid sense of the editing process, we can draw a **storyboard** of the sequence. Every time the shot or image changes, we can track it with a separate visual frame, using evocative sketches. The storyboard allows us to track both the editing and the image ownership:

Chapter Three

Close Shot: **KING HENRY** boarding ship
"Suppose that you have seen/The well-appointed king at Hampton Pier/Embark his royalty"

Pull Back to reveal: **FLEET** embarking against the rising sun
"his brave fleet/With silken streamers the young Phoebus fanning"

SPEAKING IN CLOSE-UPS: Image & Description

Pan across: **SHIP-BOYS** climbing the hempen tackle
"behold/Upon the hempen tackle ship-boys climbing"

Medium Shot: **SAILS**—fluttering against the wind
"the threaden sails,/Borne with the invisible and creeping wind"

Chapter Three

Traveling Shot: **HUGE SHIPS** moving across the waves
"Draw the huge bottoms through the furrowed sea"

Close on: **PROW of Ship** cutting through choppy waters
"Breasting the lofty surge"

SPEAKING IN CLOSE-UPS: Image & Description

Long Shot from shore: **ARMADA of Ships**
"A city on the inconstant billows dancing"

(Original illustrations by artist Arielle Jessop)

    The Chorus' camera zooms in, it zooms out, it takes in a large panoramic sweep, like the fleet of battleships glistening on the waters, or it moves in to capture a closer image, like sails fluttering against the wind. He shows the choppy waters, he pans across the ship-boys climbing the tackle. Each frame requires the performer to distinctly point it up, give it a unique vocal attack or melody.

    In contrast, vocal monotony or dullness will stop the editing process, turn the story into one undifferentiated sequence of vagueness. Again, continually shifting vocal expression and aliveness signals to the listener that the frame has changed. The speaker has a hungry desire to show the audience each image. Try it. Roll out your movie screen and try this speech, making vivid vocal distinctions with each new frame.

Making Words: Onomatopoeia

    The Chorus is a dynamic editor, as he seeks to surround us with image—and *sound*. Notice how Shakespeare provides an audio cue in the middle of the speech: "Hear the shrill whistle which doth order give/To sounds confused."

Chapter Three

Amid the cacophony of sounds, including the wind, sea, sails fluttering, and bustle of soldiers, we hear the shipmaster's shrill whistle cutting through the dissonance.

"Shrill whistle" is an example of **Onomatopoeia** (on o ma to PEE-ya) where words are *echoing or imitating natural sounds*. Onomatopoeia is the Greek term for the "making of words." *Onoma* means "word" and *poiein* means "to make." The tea kettle *hissed* its fury. The wolves *howled* at the moon. Onomatopoeia is a descriptive strategy meant to bolster the audience's *experience* of that particular word, as it draws the audience into the surround sound world of the described event. It serves the larger figure of enargia.

Actors generally do not take advantage of these kinds of audio cues for fear of transgressing the contemporary "realist" speaking style, one that inhibits the actor's adventure with words. But onomatopoeia requires the performer to re-create the sound, to take a bold approach to the making of sound. You can informatively say, "The wolves howled at the moon," or you can reach for something much more experiential and aural by saying, "The wolves howwwwled at the moon." Or a bit more subtle: "howwled at the moon." There are varying degrees of adventurousness. "Shrill whistle" is not simply a piece of audio information; it *is* the audio. It echoes the sense. Say it out loud; experiment with it and you will find its descriptive allure. Elizabethan performers were well prepared to exploit sound on stage, to mine the palpable experience embedded inside language.

Throughout his plays, Shakespeare takes bold opportunities to wed image and sound. In *Julius Caesar*, Calphurnia, Caesar's wife, warns her husband not to leave their house, fearing for his safety. She has heard a watchman describe terrifying omens that she interprets as warning signs of impending disaster. So she describes these omens, in urgent living color and sound, to her husband.

> A lioness hath whelped in the streets,
> And graves have yawn'd and yielded up their dead;
> Fierce fiery warriors fight upon the clouds
> In ranks and squadrons and right form of war,
> Which drizzled blood upon the Capitol;
> The noise of battle hurtled in the air;
> Horses did neigh, and dying men did groan,

SPEAKING IN CLOSE-UPS: Image & Description

And ghosts did shriek and squeal about the streets.
O Caesar, these things are beyond all use,
And I do fear them.

(2.2)

This is a 3-D movie in Dolby Stereo. Remember, Calphurnia wants to persuade Caesar to stay home, so she vividly describes, "before his eyes," a series of events that portend death and chaos. People believed in omens and in their prophetic power. Her graphic description places the audience in the middle of the action. The editing is swift and sharp, changing images with each line:

—A lioness hath *whelped* in the streets   [*given birth*]

—And graves have yawn'd and yielded up their dead

—Fierce fiery warriors fight upon the clouds

—In ranks and squadrons and right form of war

—Which drizzled blood upon the Capitol

A lion giving birth, dead people rising from graves, a battle in the clouds, red rain falling on the streets of Rome: This is a sequence of distinct and haunting images. Can you see them? And then Calphurnia turns on the stereo sound, using onomatopoeia to boost the aural experience:

—The noise of battle *hurtled* in the air

—Horses did *neigh*, and dying men did *groan*

—And ghosts did *shriek* and *squeal* about the streets

These are evocative words, awaiting the actor's bravery. Again, it is not enough to simply recite these operative audio words as mere concepts. These words marry sound and meaning. They embody and convey the experience of the event. The actor must *make* these words. With dying men groaning, horses neighing, and ghosts shrieking and squealing, the opportunities for courageous vocal expression are many. Now, the actor can go too far and turn the words into a showcase for sound effects. Sound can become disconnected from meaning, from the play, for that matter. This is why it is important for

Chapter Three

the performer to experiment. She can always scale back, take it down several notches.

Scaling back is not the problem. Allowing ourselves permission to test the boundaries of vocal expression *is* the problem. Giving ourselves freedom to reach inside the guts of language *is* the problem. The narrow way in which we view language restricts our choices. Once we allow language to be a dynamic thrilling vehicle of human expression, we open up a new universe of performance possibilities:

GROAN

NEIGH

SHRIEK

SQUEAL

Make these words. Go at it. Like a raucous kid in the toy room, you can have some fun and discover uncharted terrain of vocal communication. Vocalize the actual sound while still maintaining the integrity of the word. Use trial and error. Making words may feel strange or unacceptable. It's alright. Tomorrow it may feel a little more acceptable. In any case, you have the opportunity to expand your vocal range—a key attribute of the performer. You need not use onomatopoeia at every opportunity, nor should you employ it in an overtly self-conscious way. Frequently a *subtle and covert* use of this figure can provide a rich evocative layer to the process of communicating. It gives an extra jolt to the descriptive act. Making words is yet another way to draw the audience into the immediacy of your story.

Shakespeare sought to capture the "globe" and all its wonders within the magical confines of the "Wooden O." He knew the human imagination was his ultimate partner in re-creating a piece of action. The spoken word firing the imagination of an engrossed audience is a potent force, one capable of rendering the panorama of war, ships crossing the English Channel, the storming of the breach at Harfleur, the mud and stench and sound of battle.

Shakespeare apparently took no interest in publishing his plays; no script survives in his own autograph (save for a brief excerpt of *The Book of Thomas Moore*, so-called Hand D, which many scholars believe to be Shakespeare's).

SPEAKING IN CLOSE-UPS: Image & Description

He understood that his plays lived in the arena of physical action and in the sound and words that breathed life into that action. The *spoken* word, delivered to a listening audience, was his consuming passion. Together, the player and the audience could create the visual and aural landscapes that revealed a mermaid riding on a dolphin's back, singing an entrancing melody, calming the sea's unruly waters, during a midsummer night's dream.

Contemporary Stage Cinema

The flame of enargia is still alive today. It is flickering, true, but it is still burning. While the cinema of words is routinely overshadowed by the technology of image-making, there still exist opportunities, in contemporary plays, for actors to rediscover a lost art. Today, there are playwrights who explore the descriptive richness and exciting legacy of human storytelling. In their plays, actors are invited to reclaim the power of language. The dialogue is often glazed in flavored prose rather than verse, but the result is the same: Opportunities abound for the performer to paint images through the spoken word.

In Eric Overmyer's *On the Verge or The Geography of Dreaming*, three 19th-century American women adventurers, modeled on Victorian women explorers, embark on an intrepid journey into Terra Incognita, trekking into exotic locales and, step by step, into the 20th century. The play is a journey into the human imagination, seen through the multicolored lens of the ladies' use of language.

Throughout the play, the women provide travelogue journal entries, spoken directly to the audience, which chronicle their fantastical observations and experiences. "I have seen wonders in the Himalayas," begins Alexandra, as she describes watching the lama priests raise their body temperatures by "mere mental exertion."

> They would sleep all night in snowbanks. At dawn, they would douse themselves in freezing streams. Then, ice-blue and on the verge of extinction, they would sit lotus and meditate ferociously. Instantly, steam would sizzle off them in clouds, rising past their furrowed brows. In an hour, their robes would be dry as toast—and neatly pressed.

Chapter Three

Alexandra now switches locale and continues her description.

> In the blue shadow of Crystal Mountain, I watched a Bon shaman wrap himself in his black cape, fold himself thrice, become a giant origami crow, flap flap flap his wings, rise into the sky, and fly across the saffron moon.
>
> (Scene 2)

In her description, Alexandra blends physical and mystical images as she takes us into an exotic and marvelous world. Enargia is the key performance tool that can fully *realize* this kind of dialogue. It is vital that the audience follows and "sees" the visual phenomena of this journal entry. Many of the images are captivating. Some are otherworldly. And yet they are accessible to our imagination. They wed the rituals of another culture with detailed physicality. But unless we have personally spent some time hanging out with the lama priests of Tibet, we may not possess *vivid command* of these images. They are beyond our experience. To achieve the verbal ownership necessary to infuse the description with vividness and distinctness, with bravery and confidence, the actor playing Alexandra has a bit of creative research to do.

First, pull out some pictures of the Himalayas. Get acquainted with the soaring landscapes and settlements and peoples that dot this enormous expanse of geography. You are not trying to become a scholar, but you do need to anchor your descriptive work in a specific physical location. Who are the lama priests? What do they look like? What do they wear? What is the role of meditation in their lives? What is the lotus position? Find out about their daily rituals and prayers. Remember, you are striving for that "before your eyes" visual immediacy. After a while, you will begin to *see* what Alexandra sees. You will begin to visualize the specific images she uses to capture the lamas' rituals:

—**they sleep all night in snowbanks**

—**they douse themselves in freezing streams**

—**ice-blue, they sit lotus and meditate ferociously**

—**steam sizzles off them in clouds**

SPEAKING IN CLOSE-UPS: Image & Description

> —steam rises past furrowed brows
> —their robes dry as toast and neatly pressed

This speech is a wonderful cinematic excursion for the actor. Notice also the editing of this passage. Each line signals a new image, a change of frame or screen. The voice tracks these changes of frame. From snowbanks to freezing streams to lotus position to steam sizzling to furrowed brows to dry robes, each image has to be brought onto the screen—separately, in close-ups, so that the audience can enjoy it, partake in its mystery and beauty.

In the second part, Alexandra focuses on the Bon shaman of Crystal Mountain. The same preparatory research is required here, of course. Most of us have not seen a Bon shaman transform himself into an origami crow and fly across a saffron moon, but like the phantasmagoric characters of Shakespeare's *Midsummer Night's Dream*, the performer must reach high into the visual stratosphere, to describe the extraordinary in a concrete, fully fleshed, palpable way. The visual scale is different, but not the commitment needed to execute the imagery. Spend some time with the Bon shaman, watch his transformation into the origami crow, and you will summon the unapologetic brashness to make your audience see the crow "flap flap flap" its wings as it lifts off into the sky. Be specific. Generalized speaking is always the enemy of the actor on stage, never more so than in describing the richly attired events of this world—and the one beyond.

In Naomi Iizuka's ensemble play, *Language of Angels*, a story about a group of young people reconstructing the events surrounding the mysterious disappearance of a friend, the author uses a heady mix of imagery floating between the waking and dreaming worlds. In this speech, Michael, talking to some young women in a parking lot at night, describes a surreal late-night drive along a desert highway:

> I could barely keep my eyes from closing, driving all that darkness for so long, can't see but for the double-line, we coulda been in deepest space, a dream of space playing along the backs of my eyes—half asleep, it all begins to look the same, shades of purple bleeding into black—but then, then, we saw it up ahead, tiny lights raining down from the sky, bright and fast, so bright, and then it's

Chapter Three

> gone. It looked just like fireworks, like some kinda show, Vegas Strip, snowflakes and flowers sparkling in the sky, each one bigger brighter than the next, everybody in that car that night going ooh aah, like they had just seen something, something beautiful.
>
> (Part 2)

One of the intriguing aspects of this play is that much of it takes place in relative darkness or in dimly lit environments, including in caves during the first half. Against this dark background the actor's voice becomes the primary flame for illuminating the story. The audience must rely, almost exclusively, on the actor's command of images, including the imagery of darkness, as the story unfolds. Each actor's voice is like a beacon of light, revealing shiny bits of scenery.

Michael's speech begins in drowsy darkness; his camera's point of view catches the car's headlights illuminating the road's double line. We see an endless succession of line swallowed into night. The character then describes the night as "deepest space" and as "shades of purple bleeding into black." Both on stage in the shadowy parking lot and "in" the car, the audience is now enveloped by darkness. But then, suddenly, an exploding meteor shower shatters this dark cyclorama and lights up our imaginations:

> **we saw it up ahead**
>
> **tiny lights raining down from the sky**
>
> **bright and fast**

Michael compares the meteor bombardment to a fireworks display, the Vegas Strip, describing the lights as "snowflakes and flowers sparkling in the sky." This sequence is a dramatic visual treat for an audience. It reveals the potential of enargia in the hands of a fiercely committed actor, one who wants the audience to see this cosmic lightshow, in the middle of the desert, lost in night, swerving along an endless highway.

One of the most evocative opportunities for enargia in 20th-century theater occurs in Noel Coward's play *Quadrille*. Coward's characters are more known for uncorking witty one-liners, while dangling cocktails or cigarettes, than for presenting rich visual panoramas. And yet Axel, a railway magnate, takes us on an unforgettable journey across America. "Come to my country

SPEAKING IN CLOSE-UPS: Image & Description

one day," he tells Serena, a striking British woman who is curious about the new world and for whom he has developed a budding attraction. Axel then turns on his "film," revealing a variety of majestic landscapes as seen from the particular vantage of the caboose's brakeman.

> There he sits, hour in hour out, watching the trees marching along and the cinders and earth and sands of America slipping away beneath the wheels. He can watch the sun set over the gentle farmlands of Wisconsin and rise over the interminable prairies of Nebraska and Illinois and Kansas. Those flat, flat lands bring the sky so low that on clear nights you can almost feel that you are rattling along through the stars. It is rougher going in the mountains where there are sharp curves and steep gradients and the locomotive strains and gasps and fills the air with steam and sparks; tunnels close round you, infernos of noise and sulphurous smoke, then suddenly you are in the open and can breathe again and there are snow-covered peaks towering above you and pine forests and the sound of waterfalls. Over it all and through it all, the familiar, reassuring noise of the train; a steady beat on the level stretches when the wheels click over the joints in the rails but changing into wilder rhythms when you clatter over bridges and crossings and intersections. The railroad is my dream, ma'am, the whole meaning of my life, my pride and all my hopes for the future.

(2.3)

Would you like to hop aboard this train and see America? Would you like to fully absorb the process of travel rather than simply arrive at your destination? This speech puts us on the train, sits us next to the brakeman, gives us a window seat onto the world, as we watch the changes in topography and light, feel the wheels rattle beneath us, smell the locomotive smoke, and hear the chug and roar of the engine. It's a total sensory experience. It starts in the caboose and ends in our imagination. It achieves an astonishing descriptive immediacy that the actor can exploit. To do so, let's activate our editing machine and our storyboard to give the actor a frame-by-frame clarity. Climb aboard that caboose and take in—

Chapter Three

"the trees marching along…"

"…and the cinders and earth and sands of America slipping away beneath the wheels."

SPEAKING IN CLOSE-UPS: Image & Description

"the sun set over the gentle farmlands of Wisconsin…"

"and rise over the interminable prairies of Nebraska…"

Chapter Three

"Those flat, flat lands bring the sky so low that on clear nights you can almost feel that you are rattling along through the stars…"

"It is rougher going in the mountains where there are sharp curves…"

SPEAKING IN CLOSE-UPS: Image & Description

"and steep gradients…"

"the locomotive strains and gasps and fills the air with steam and sparks…"

Chapter Three

"tunnels close round you…"

"then suddenly you are in the open…"

SPEAKING IN CLOSE-UPS: Image & Description

"snow-covered peaks towering above you…"

(Original illustrations by artist Arielle Jessop)

Notice how Axel dramatically edits the screen images, from farms to prairies, from flatlands to mountains, from tunnels to wide-open spaces with snow-covered peaks. Again, the actor's voice commands the editing process, signaling a brave new image with each shift in tone or stress. Notice, too, how Axel provides sound cues, describing the train as "rattling along," and he follows the steady "click" of the wheels over the rail joints, and then picks up wild rhythmic intensity as the train "clatters" over a bridge or crossing. We also hear "infernos of noise" in the tunnels, the sound of waterfalls, and the "gasp" of steam spewing into the air, as the engine "sparks" and strains its way up the steep mountain gradients. We feel the train chugging along and we even smell the sulfur of its smoke.

Axel wants Serena to visit his country. So his tour of the American heartland gives her a front-row seat so that she can be fully immersed in the journey, enveloped by the adventure, following the train's progress across the varying landscapes.

He does not merely provide information; he provides an experience.

Chapter Three

The actor, like Axel, can strive to give his listener that same experience. Before he can place her on that caboose, the actor first needs to "ride the rails," tracking each image and change of scenery, getting each image or sound inside his camera. Contemporary stage enargia, like its classical predecessor, works with the same strategy: Own the images, edit, speak in close-ups.

Two Editors

Finally, two characters can share and build a physical description together. They can feed off each other's remembrance of a particular event, helping one another bring each image alive, filling it in with increasing color and contours. In Lucy Kirkwood's *Hedda*, a contemporary adaptation of Henrik Ibsen's *Hedda Gabler*, set in London, Hedda and her ill-destined soulmate Eli recall "that day," a momentous afternoon and evening that brought them sensuously and dangerously close to one another. Eli, anxious to reconnect with the bewitching woman he remembers, prods Hedda's memory, inspiring her to help him re-create the events of *that day*. "We'd been drinking since noon," he says, noting that they "dived into the river to cool down." Hedda accepts his invitation.

> HEDDA: …you pulled me in after you.
> ELI: I tried not to look at you through the wet cotton
> HEDDA: You gave me your dry shirt to wear
> ELI: Hung your dress on a tree
> HEDDA: Watched it steam…
> ELI: Then I carried you up the towpath on my back
> HEDDA: Ivy leaves caught in your hair
> ELI: Pondweed really, but you said it was
> HEDDA: Ivy leaves. Wound through your hair
> ELI: The sun still high
> HEDDA: It was low
> ELI: It was high
> HEDDA: The sky was turning pink
> ELI: Was it?
> HEDDA: Like fish blood

SPEAKING IN CLOSE-UPS: Image & Description

> ELI: You're right. It was sunset
> HEDDA: The end of an exquisite day
>
> (Act Two)

They suddenly remember that this afternoon turned into an adventurous night at a dance bar. In overlapping dialogue, Eli recalls Hedda moving "like water," while Hedda summons the "sticky floors" and "condensed sweat dripping" from the ceiling and the "UV lights and cheap shots." Eli remembers a guy hitting on Hedda.

> ELI: That kid tried to come on to you
> HEDDA: Got in my way, I just wanted to dance
> ELI: You stubbed your cigarette out on his neck
> HEDDA: He screamed like a girl

Both Hedda and Eli snatch visual fragments to reenact the events of that day. They play off each other. The images are spiked with intoxicating emotional connotation, making the enargia all the more potent. Suddenly these two rebellious characters are transported back to the river, a dress hung on a tree, a pink sky. At night, the images quicken: dancing, sticky floors, UV lights, condensed sweat, a cigarette, a scream. The images, in a way, rekindle the relationship for a brief spell, allowing the two characters to remember their feelings and attraction for one another, the moments and secrets they shared. This dialogue requires a commitment from both actors, an uncommon desire to vividly paint the memories for each other—and for us.

TAKING STOCK

We have seen how the spoken word can evoke striking visual power. Once this awareness is present, then the frame of *expectation* suddenly changes: What is the human performer capable of conjuring? If you do not know—or believe—the human voice and creative imagination can re-create graphic and wondrous images "before our eyes" then you create a safe and small frame of expectation. You send generalized "postcards" to an audience. It is not a

Chapter Three

question of talent. It is a question of awareness—and brave confidence. If you suddenly see that the human performer can re-create an entire montage of visual cues to a rapt audience then you have built a much larger frame of expectation. You can now display tall "billboards" to an audience. Seemingly out of scale to the painter up on the scaffolding, the billboard image looks just right to the motorist cruising by. Like the painter on that large canvas, the actor can reach for a more courageous and powerful sense of expression, one that challenges our restrictive contemporary casualness of speech.

The images and descriptive passages in this chapter rely on a more adventurous vocal scale—and commitment. They rely on the performer magnifying the image through the voice, in close-ups. They rely on the performer's ability to edit, making clear distinctions between one image and the next. We have seen that enargia, like the *Iliad*'s Narrator or Shakespeare's Chorus, like Alexandra or Axel, does not settle for a summary of an event, a casual approximation; it wants to get *inside* the event, onto the field of battle, inside the soldier's chariot, aboard the ships with King Henry's men, alongside the meditating priest lamas, riding the rails with the train brakeman. Enargia wants to put you in the arena of action.

Shakespeare and his contemporaries did not have our modern terms from film to describe effective imagery. Cutaways and close-ups, of course, were not part of their experience. But the principles underlying these modern applications did in fact exist. Great speakers practiced making vivid switches from one specific image to the next. That's editing. The ear and imagination followed the editing cues. Shakespeare could observe the exquisite "close-up" of one artist's portrait painting and contrast it with the "long" perspective of another artist's landscape painting. For centuries, speakers and audiences understood that words could convey graphic perspective and detail.

For several millennia, people understood that human "electricity" powered the engine of storytelling.

So today we can adapt the technical language and artistry of electronic media to further our own investigation into human power. The theater is ultimately generated by this latter source.

When we speak in verbal close-ups, we summon an energy not bound by contemporary technology, a power not defined by iPhones and widescreen

SPEAKING IN CLOSE-UPS: Image & Description

smart TVs. Indeed, we tap into a source not fueled by any electronic device, one that emanates from our very selves. Its origin lies in the vast pools of our fathomless imagination and in our ability to give voice—and word—to the pictures we see in our mind's eye. Today's actor can celebrate this amazing attribute and reclaim it for the 21st-century stage. The scene is set. Speak your movie.

Chapter Four

MAKING CONNECTIONS: Metaphor

The ordinary doesn't move us. The commonplace sedates us. Literal description keeps us tethered to a mundane plane of safe and predictable outcomes. In our perpetual hunger to explain our actions or to describe some fascinating fragment of our world, we reach for something beyond the commonplace. We reach for something that sparks our mind into motion and infuses our body with energy. We crave movement, in thought, in imagination, in the body—and in language. Movement, by its very nature, lifts us off our mark, takes us to another location, one we perhaps have not visited before, a place of wide-eyed discovery and newness.

Language is a transporter, a high-speed magic carpet ride that zooms us to faraway worlds and unexpected landscapes. One of the ways the actor can activate this transporter is to make connections with language. These connections, or associations, require imaginative movement, coaxing us to travel from one side of the connection to the other. In that act of travel comes the reward.

Let's take a seat on the magic carpet. How do we get it going? We need some fueling words. Let's imagine Albert has been working on a difficult physics problem, and suddenly he finds the elusive solution: $E=MC^2$. Now, Albert may simply exclaim, "I've solved the problem!" Fine. That statement occurs many times in any given day. But perhaps Albert, exalting in his accomplishment, sees a crack in the universe and dares to reach for an expression that elicits a different kind of response: "I've wrestled this opponent to the ground!" In this statement, Albert has made a connection, between solving and wrestling. The sentence activates the listener's magic carpet as it travels from one side (solving a problem) to the other (wrestling an opponent), comparing the two in a flash of mental activity. The information is the same as in the straightforward linear version—"I've solved the problem"—but the

MAKING CONNECTIONS: Metaphor

strategy is quite different. One, as we shall see, is *active* in its energy, the other *static*; one comparative, the other linear. The active, comparative statement takes us into the wide, open country of metaphor. For the actor, there is no better place to be.

METAPHOR
The Connector

Metaphor (MET a for), an ancient Greek word meaning "transference," *finds a connection between two dissimilar things and compares them.* The connection is direct and "taken for granted," as the *attributes of one thing are transferred to another thing.* In "I've wrestled this opponent [problem] to the ground," the physical attributes of wrestling are *transferred*—implicitly—to the mental state of solving problems. In vivid pictures, the listener suddenly sees the person facing off against the Opponent/Problem, circling it cautiously, suddenly lunging at it, grabbing it, putting it in a headlock, taking its feet out from under it, driving it to the mat—and pinning it for the ten count. The listener's mind rapidly moves between the *source* ("problem solving," the subject to which attributes are ascribed) and the *vehicle*, to borrow I. A. Richards' term, which provides the basis for movement and comparison—in this case, wrestling.

Liveliness and Surprise

Metaphor enhances our communication by providing, as Aristotle pointed out in his foundational treatise on rhetoric, an element of *liveliness* and *surprise*. "Liveliness"—a translation of the Greek term *energounta* (itself related to our English word "energy")—is attained by placing things directly "before the eyes of the audience," by using phrases that show things in a "state of activity" (*Rhetoric*, 3.11, trans. by Lane Cooper). The listener desires to "see things." Movement and rapid motion, he concludes, are essential to transference, as metaphor imbues objects with life. Liveliness in turn is enhanced by the element of "Surprise" (a form of *apate* or deception): The listener, who

Chapter Four

expected a very different statement, is suddenly made aware of an unexpected new idea or concept. His mind absorbs the surprising idea and is delighted with a newfound insight.

We may not have thought of problem solving on the same plane as wrestling before, we may not have made that connection, and so the movement between the two sides creates a kind of unexpected surprise, a payoff of delight. A state of activity—the liveliness—is also triggered: One cannot "see" the mental state of solving problems, but one can vividly "see" a wrestler pinning his opponent to the mat. Metaphor provides a palpable image to what otherwise would be an ordinary piece of information. It lights up our minds and entices our active engagement through its method of transference, its movement. How can the actor take strong advantage of metaphor in her speaking? How can the performer generate "movement" in his communication? What payoff does metaphor yield in a live stage performance? Before we can answer these questions, we must first hike up our awareness of metaphor in our reading and in our listening. We must also increase our appreciation for how metaphor reenergizes the world by its ability to seek out unusual or unexpected connections. That gives us a place to start. Once we recognize a metaphorical pattern and appreciate its creative power, we can deliver its exciting payoff to a scene partner and to the audience. So, three steps:

◊ **Awareness**
◊ **Appreciation**
◊ **Delivery**

Our magic carpet is hovering, ready for passengers. Wanna ride?

Metaphorical "Run," or: Follow the Bouncing Ball

In Shakespeare's history play, *King John*, the young French Prince Lewis is urged by Cardinal Pandulph, an emissary from the Pope, to attack the apostate forces of King John. England's King John, besides claiming territories on French soil, refuses to recognize the authority of the Pope. Prince Lewis, inspired by the cardinal from Rome, raises an army, marches through

MAKING CONNECTIONS: Metaphor

the French countryside, and prepares to meet the English forces in a decisive battle. Cardinal Pandulph, in a last-minute diplomatic reversal, suddenly visits Lewis and orders him to disarm and disband: King John, in an unexpected conversion, has agreed to accept the authority of the Pope. There is now no necessity for war, Pandulph explains. Lewis is stunned. How could the cardinal, who earlier urged war, now preach the gospel of peace? A defiant Lewis refuses to submit to the *dictat* from Rome and answers the cardinal in vivid terms.

> Your breath first kindled the dead coal of war
> Between this chastis'd kingdom and myself
> And brought in matter that should feed this fire,
> And now 'tis far too huge to be blown out
> With that same weak wind which enkindl'd it.
>
> (5.1)

This language creates movement across an implied connection between two subjects: Idea and Fire. Lewis does not simply say, "This was your idea, wasn't it? And now that you have given me this idea, I cannot ignore its powerful influence. There is no turning back." He does not opt for this linear version. It lacks the spark and motion and surprise he requires. It does not move us. Lewis instead reaches for *transference*. He transfers the vehicle of "Fire" to the source of "Idea." In Lewis' version, the cardinal's idea becomes a three-alarm fire that, once started, grows into a raging inferno. That puff of breath that first fanned the "coal of war" cannot now extinguish its blazing aftermath. Lewis creates a striking analogy, one that animates the imagination and mind, captivating the listener.

Let's look, specifically, at how Lewis builds this metaphor of Fire and how it may be of service to the actor. Lewis creates a classic metaphorical "run." That is, he creates links in a chain, notes in a melody. If the chain is Fire, then we can identify the words that provide the links. We can follow the bouncing ball:

> Your **breath** first **kindled** the dead **coal** of war
> Between this chastis'd kingdom and myself
> And brought in **matter** that should **feed this fire**,

Chapter Four

> And now 'tis far too huge to be **blown out**
> With that same **weak wind** which **enkindl'd** it.

The highlighted words carry the imagery of fire and, together, create a metaphorical "run." In the context of the third line, the word "matter" signified "fuel" in Shakespeare's day. Wind, kindling, coal, fuel, blown out—all contribute to our fire. Every line feeds the metaphorical run, except the second line, which is a straightforward linear one.

To get a handle on this run—and the evocative imagery and movement it evokes—the actor can simply start by stressing or emphasizing the operative words. He can follow the bouncing ball and accent only those words which build the fire: breath, kindled, coal, matter, etc. Let it be mechanical in the beginning, it's OK. We are simply pulling out the words in order to inspect them, appreciate them, taste them. We want to get those words of transference into our tongue and imagination. By mechanically stressing the operative words, we are searing the run into our consciousness and tracking its progress across the terrain.

The actor, much like a musician, is playing a scale, getting familiar with the specific notes that build the run, and not worrying about the mechanical nature of that scale.

The scale is an interim step. It is not an end in itself. The actor is building heightened awareness of how the metaphor is moving. After the scale is engrained and mastered, the actor can relax the speaking—and release the fully charged operative words into the larger context of the whole speech. A hint of highlight may remain. In performance, the actor is not giving the audience a lesson in metaphor. However, the actor is drawing the audience into a story, asking them to follow a tale about a fire grown too big and inviting them to rapidly make a connection to an idea grown too strong.

This is why the Neapolitan philosopher Giambattista Vico (1688–1744) called metaphor a condensed **fable**. It's a tale with a parallel undercurrent. "There once was a reckless man who loved to play with matches, boasting that he could always master the fire. One day he lit a match, put it to paper, blew on the flame, poured oil on it, watched the flames leap high into the air, suddenly the flames were too big and high, consuming everything, he tried vainly to blow the flames out but the fire kept growing and growing...."

Fables strike deep within the listener. This one is called "No Going Back." Fables activate a sense of play and image and fantasy. They entice our listening, draw us in, and solicit our participation. We are not merely listening; we are participating. That's the strong allure that metaphor features. Like the fable, metaphor creates movement between the source and the vehicle. We know that the story is not really about Fire but about a process that cannot be stopped. It's also about Arrogance and Control. Hop on Aladdin's supersonic carpet and travel between the two sides of the connection, the actor implicitly says to the listener, both Cardinal Pandulph and the audience.

Metaphor also relies on action ("state of activity") and image. We have all seen a fire start from a small source and grow into a mighty force, one that adopts its own destiny. We cannot *see* an idea growing in our mind, but we can watch a fire gather force—and compare it to the idea. Prince Lewis wants the cardinal to fully understand that his army's march against King John cannot be stopped. It's too late. Lewis wants the cardinal to see a small flame turn into a raging fire. In this sense metaphor borrows a page from the figure of Enargia (see Chapter 3). Like the descriptive mechanism of enargia, metaphor also strives to summon an image "before the eyes" of the listener. Action—and its servant, Image—constitutes the "liveliness" that Aristotle prized. We bring lifeless things alive, he said, when we transfer them, move them, into a state of activity. A fire is a state of activity that can be observed.

In practicing the mechanical scale, stressing the words of fire, the actor is not only tracking the progress of a thematic run but also reinforcing the "liveliness" of those words. He is getting the image into his body and mind. Even after relaxing the speech for performance mode, the actor may still choose to give the operative words a slight vocal *push* in order to sustain the active imagery that they evoke.

Theater makers, both directors and actors alike, often underappreciate the role of metaphor in a text. Metaphor is not window dressing, a fanciful exercise in flowery language. It is a powerful indispensable element of the production. How a character makes connections in the world speaks volumes about that person. It reveals personality and the active working of the mind. Moreover, the language of transference creates a different kind of meaning; it calls forth a very different kind of communication. It engages the listener by

Chapter Four

directly soliciting imaginative participation. And it creates wonder that a connection has been found that that the listener perhaps has not anticipated or expected

Look at Queen Margaret's speech, in Shakespeare's *Henry VI, Part 2*, to her husband, King Henry, warning him of the growing political power of his uncle, the Duke of Gloucester. Her husband, she fears, is too trusting, too naïve in his assessment of his uncle. Margaret begins the speech with a series of antithetical pairings, contrasting disturbing changes in Gloucester's behavior. Once mild, affable, and submissive, Gloucester has lately become insolent, haughty, and proud. Next in line for the crown and possessing a "rancorous mind," Gloucester poses a direct threat to Henry. Margaret, in straightforward language, advises Henry to bar his uncle from the Royal Council. She then notes that Gloucester is gaining support among the common people.

> By flattery hath he won the commons' hearts;
> And when he please to make commotion,
> 'Tis to be fear'd they all will follow him.

The language is essentially nonfigurative and straightforward. But then Margaret shifts into a dramatically different kind of communication.

> Now 'tis the spring, and weeds are shallow-rooted;
> Suffer them now, and they'll overgrow the garden,
> And choke the herbs for want of husbandry.   [want=lack]

Suddenly we are in a different place. Queen Margaret has transferred the conversation *into the garden*, so to speak. Margaret makes a connection so she can enhance her message by its liveliness and surprise. In this gardening metaphor, the Duke of Gloucester is directly compared to weeds that can take over the garden, King Henry's kingdom, and kill the herbs, King Henry's supporters (or perhaps King Henry himself). King Henry is implicitly cast as the caretaker or gardener, one who must act quickly to uproot the "shallow-rooted" weeds before they "overgrow the garden." He must not lack "husbandry," a term signifying the art of cultivating plants and soil, as well as careful management. Henry must therefore be decisive. So let's follow the bouncing ball:

MAKING CONNECTIONS: Metaphor

> Now 'tis the **spring**, and **weeds** are **shallow-rooted**;
> Suffer them now, and they'll **overgrow** the **garden**,
> And choke the **herbs** for want of **husbandry**.

Each of the highlighted words contributes to the run that comprises this gardening metaphor. There is an ominous underscore to Queen Margaret's *fable* about a garden left unattended.

> *Once upon a time there was a careless king who had a lovely little garden. He didn't seem to notice that the weeds were spreading across the soil, killing the herbs, choking the plants. By the time he noticed or roused himself into action, it was too late. His beautiful garden had become a foul tangle of underbrush. The king had been foolish, unaware, a poor gardener. Despondent, he realized that he should have uprooted those evil weeds while there was still time.*

Queen Margaret's cautionary tale leaves open the interpretation associated with uprooting weeds. Is she urging the banishment of Gloucester? Or is she urging something more sinister—the permanent removal of his uncle? She will leave the final interpretation to Henry.

Margaret's connection makes the listener prick up his ears. Henry may not have connected gardening with political headhunting before. It is the surprise that metaphor brings that makes the hearer receive a jolt of illumination. This jolt pleases the listener, as Aristotle reminded us, gives him fresh knowledge, a sense that he has found a new way to interpret human action. The actor playing Margaret should fully appreciate this illumination because it will lead to more interesting acting choices on stage. Let's look at a larger chunk of her speech, so that we can see how the actor can deliver a payoff to this metaphorical run.

> First note that he is near you in descent,
> And should you fall, he is the next will mount.
> Me seemeth then it is no policy,
> Respecting what a rancorous mind he bears
> And his advantage following your decease,
> That he should come about your royal person,

Chapter Four

> Or be admitted to your Highness' Council.
> By flattery hath he won the commons' hearts;
> And when he please to make commotion,
> 'Tis to be fear'd they all will follow him.
> *Now 'tis the spring, and weeds are shallow-rooted;*
> *Suffer them now, and they'll overgrow the garden,*
> *And choke the herbs for want of husbandry.*
>
> (3.1)

This change in font allows us to see the contrast between the metaphorical language and the nonfigurative language preceding it. An actor can take advantage of this difference, accenting the element of surprise and liveliness associated with the last three lines. The "gardening" lines ask for a change in vocal tone, rhythm, stress. They sing a different melody. If the preceding lines are in the key of G major, for instance, the sudden switch into transferred language can be spoken in D minor, with its own rhythm and tone.

This vocal change is not an arbitrary one or a purely technical one. It is a character-driven, necessary change, one rooted in the actor's *intention*. Margaret wants to find a more effective way to rouse the king, she wants to make him see the peril surrounding him, and so she finds a connection, a fable that warns of weeds spreading, time running out, and the need for rooting out the underbrush. Henry cannot see growing political subterfuge and conspiracy in his midst, Margaret knows, so she makes him see a concrete physical image. It is an image the king had not anticipated.

Actors spend many studio hours discussing how they can affect—or connect with—their scene partner in a play, primarily looking into psychological needs and creating a vast *sub*text to the scene. That's fine. But what about the language itself? The actual *surface* of the text? Margaret's gardening language signals a ratcheting up of persuasive intent, a strong desire to spur the king into action. An actor can play the language to achieve that purpose. Margaret can make Henry see the despoiled garden, his kingdom. She can make him realize that the weeds are shallow and that he must act to remove them—quickly. That's why a change into D minor signals a change into a vivid form of one-on-one persuasion. Try Margaret's speech aloud. Play with it. See if you can discover a needful change when you tell a tale of a king and his garden.

MAKING CONNECTIONS: Metaphor

Some actors gloss over a metaphorical run in their speaking, unsure of its importance, uncomfortable with its dramatic imagery. They privately fear that this language is too indulgent, too stylized, not lifelike, so they rush through it and breathe easier once they get to the open meadow of linear language, their comfort zone. In doing so, they miss the very point of this kind of verbal expression—a journey into the wildest and most scenic landscapes of human persuasion.

The metaphor contains the excitement of discovery and new perspective that electrifies an idea or piece of communication.

In the bustling marketplace of Shakespeare's world, the characters spurn ordinary humdrum language because it doesn't produce the lightning bolt of surprise and vividness that they require. The world, they insist, is too wondrous a place for casual expression. So they seek out movement in language, metaphor, transference, a way to lift the listener off the predictable and into the lively buzzing places. They glide that magical carpet right to your doorstep and dare you to go for a spin.

Wilde "Run"

In Oscar Wilde's play, *An Ideal Husband*, the Machiavellian Mrs. Cheveley threatens to expose Sir Robert Chiltern, a government minister who, in a youthful moment of weakness, secretly sold a Cabinet secret for a large sum of money. She will expose him unless he backs her shady financial scheme. Her terms of blackmail are buttressed by lively, deliberate word choices.

> For the moment I am your enemy. I admit it! And I am much stronger than you are. The big battalions are on my side. You have a splendid position, but it is your splendid position that makes you so vulnerable. You can't defend it! And I am in attack.
> (Act 2)

A cunning run. Mrs. Cheveley presents a battlefield, one where her powerful armies will overwhelm Sir Robert's "position." Note that she cleverly plays

Chapter Four

on the two meanings of this word: military defense and social status. It is Sir Robert's high social status, his position, that makes him so impotent or susceptible to her strong offensive. Her forces will conquer, his will capitulate. The military terms array themselves along the front lines of her strategy:

big battalions – splendid position – vulnerable – defend – attack

Mrs. Cheveley, like many of Oscar Wilde's characters, combines a sense of danger with a canny verbal flair. It's a potent mix. This combination provides the actor with a critical *distance*, a way to make a strong point without pushing it emotionally because the language is shouldering so much of the work. The words of transference pack a powerful punch, lessening the need for the actor to overly emote or hammer an idea. In case Sir Robert doesn't fully grasp his futile state, his vulnerable position, the military images make it more vivid, graphically illustrating his looming defeat.

Playing in the Same Key, or: Verbal Tango

Two characters can share the same metaphor. They can activate a robust movement by transferring their dialogue onto another level. One character makes a connection, establishes a "key," and then the other character "reads" the connection, responds in the same key. In this way a metaphor is passed back and forth and developed, like two musicians flirting with an evolving melody. This kind of dialogue requires astute listening and a precision in speaking and offers exciting interplay between two performers.

John Vanbrugh's exquisite play, *The Relapse*, like many Restoration comedies, features numerous scenes where two characters must stay in tune with each other in order to release the wit and intrigue of the dialogue. The play's charisma and appeal derives from this interplay. In one scene Amanda is discussing her husband with a scheming friend, Berinthia, who is attempting to find a crack in Amanda's fidelity. Despite her husband's past philandering, Amanda now believes in his reformation and declares her unshakable allegiance to him.

MAKING CONNECTIONS: Metaphor

AMANDA: Fie, fie, Berinthia, you would indeed alarm me, could you incline me to a thought that all the merit of mankind combined could shake the tender love I bear my husband. No, he sits triumphant in my heart, and nothing can dethrone him.

BERINTHIA: But should he abdicate again, do you think you should preserve the vacant throne ten tedious winters more in hopes of his return?

(Act 2)

In this short example, Amanda establishes a political metaphor by the use of the word "dethrone." She implicitly compares her husband to a king who sits triumphant in her heart, incapable of being challenged or dethroned. Berinthia pounces on the imagery and responds with the word "abdicate," a political term that denotes a monarch's formal relinquishing, or giving up, the throne and its responsibilities. A very clever response! In this context, "abdicate" is associated with infidelity—cheating on one's spouse. Berinthia then injects the phrase "vacant throne" for good measure. Will Amanda, she asks figuratively, continue to stand by an unfaithful husband should he cheat again?

For this dialogue to work in performance, the actors must *stress* and *inflect* the operative—or metaphorical—words. By using changes in vocal pitch and stress on key words, the actors unleash the dazzling wit, stay in tune with each other, and allow the audience to relish the language of transference.

AMANDA: No, he sits triumphant in my heart and nothing can **dethrone** him.

BERINTHIA: But should he **abdicate** again, do you think you should preserve the **vacant throne** ten tedious winters more in hopes of his return?

It takes two to tango and this is especially true when two performers "step together" as they develop a metaphor. Amanda must *set up* the dominant metaphor "dethrone" so that Berinthia can *play off it* with "abdicate." Otherwise, the language is lost on the actors and the audience. In rehearsal, the actors can mechanically exaggerate the words of transference as a way of

Chapter Four

ingraining the metaphorical exchange. In performance, these key words will still be given accented treatment, albeit with less hammered emphasis. This kind of language openly invites the actors to play it. It is too composed for actors to ignore it. Listen to what happens when two actors do not play in the same key, striking random chords by accenting words that do not carry the King-Throne-Fidelity connections.

> AMANDA: No, **he** sits triumphant in my heart and **nothing** can dethrone him.
> BERINTHIA: But should **he** abdicate again, do you think you should preserve the vacant throne **ten tedious winters** more in hopes of his return?

Could someone even follow this exchange? The meaning is smothered right along with the metaphor. Personal pronouns rarely *carry the money*, and yet they are frequently hammered by many young actors—and some older ones—in the American theater. Why shine a light on weak inoperative words when you are surrounded by the goldmine of metaphor? In another scenario, Amanda may indeed set up Berinthia by inflecting **dethrone**, but Berinthia may not respond in the same key: She might accent the word **again** over "abdicate." In both cases, an opportunity is lost. A piece of the play is lost. Its magic slips away.

Tango Deluxe

For a much longer and exhilarating treatment of metaphorical exchange, let's take a look at a scene between Sir Loveless, Amanda's husband, and Berinthia, his wife's supposed friend. Loveless, after an initial phase of constrained fidelity, is about to suffer a *relapse* in this secretive encounter with the enchanting Berinthia.

> BERINTHIA: What makes you look so thoughtful, sir? I hope you are not **ill**?
> LOVELESS: I was debating, madam, whether I was so or not, and that was it which made me look so thoughtful.
> BERINTHIA: Is it then so hard a matter to decide? I thought all

MAKING CONNECTIONS: Metaphor

	people had been acquainted with their own *bodies*, though few people know their own *minds*.
LOVELESS:	What if the **distemper** I suspect be in the mind?
BERINTHIA:	Why, then I'll undertake to **prescribe** a **cure**.
LOVELESS:	Alas, you undertake you know not what.
BERINTHIA:	So far at least then allow me to be a **physician**.
LOVELESS:	Nay, I'll allow you so yet farther; for I have reason to believe, should I put myself into your hands you would **increase my distemper**.
BERINTHIA:	Perhaps I might have reasons from the **College** not to be too quick in your **cure**, but 'tis possible I might find ways to give you often **ease**, sir.
LOVELESS:	Were I but sure of that, I'd quickly **lay my case** before you.
BERINTHIA:	Whether you are sure of it or no, what risk do you run in trying?
LOVELESS:	Oh, a very great one.
BERINTHIA:	How?
LOVELESS:	You might betray my **distemper** to my wife.
BERINTHIA:	And so lose all my **practice**.
LOVELESS:	Will you then keep my secret?

(3.2, bold italics mine)

What a tango! If you want to dance with your scene partner, work on this scene and you will quickly learn some hot new steps. Berinthia establishes the connection to health by introducing the first dance step, the word "ill" at the top of the scene. Loveless picks up on the theme and introduces a counter-step, the word "distemper" (disease) a few lines later. Berinthia expands on this idea by casting herself as the physician and Loveless as the patient. Doctor and patient, mistress and husband, are now connected in this metaphorical dance. The doctor must find a cure to the patient's suffering, although the patient fears a quick all-out cure may worsen his disease. The doctor may consult the "College" (of Physicians) to find a slow-working incremental remedy, while the patient is willing to "lay his case," describe his symptoms, should the doctor provide some temporary "ease."

Chapter Four

Almost every line requires the actor to pay astute attention to the verbal surface, to listen to the scene partner's previous line and then counter one "step" with another "step." Again, the operative words really need to be played up, served up, using **vocal inflection**, **stress**, and smart **rhythmic elements**, to highlight the interplay. (Rhythmic elements may include, for example, a quick pause or *hitch* before an operative word, which is answered by the other actor.) The actors, together, dance this dialogue as it pirouettes across the ballroom. *This dialogue does not activate subtext. It promotes attention to surface text.* Its meaning resides in the very words themselves.

True, Loveless and Berinthia are distinct characters, with underlying intentions, but they convey their desires by overtly resorting to devices of verbal wit to harness the communicative power of words. They rely on words to release their feelings, designs—and *enjoyment*. Yes, in the Restoration period of the English stage, pleasure and play were viewed as key ingredients of human motive and behavior.

Berinthia and Loveless are not finished with their verbal tango. Loveless goes on to describe his symptoms to his doctor, noting that since he saw her at the theater, his "heart began to pant," his "limbs to tremble," his "blood grew thin," and his "pulse beat quick." Loveless then fires off a military metaphorical run to describe his weakening defense in the face of Berinthia's ravishing onslaught.

> 'Tis true, some small **recruits** of resolution
> My manhood brought to my assistance,
> And by their help I **made a stand** awhile,
> But found at last your **arrows** flew so thick
> They could not fail to **pierce** me,
> So **left the field**,
> And **fled** for **shelter** to Amanda's arms.

The battlefield terminology aptly conveys Loveless' surrender on the romantic front. The scene continues with more diagnosis and prescription.

> LOVELESS: What think you of these **symptoms**, pray?
> BERINTHIA: **Feverish**, every one of 'em. But what **relief**, pray, did your wife afford?

MAKING CONNECTIONS: Metaphor

LOVELESS: Why, instantly she let me **blood** [*drawing off blood was standard treatment for fevers*], which for the present much assuaged my **flame**. But when I saw you, out it burst again and raged with greater fury than before. Nay, since you now appear, 'tis so increased, that in a moment if you do not help me I shall, whilst you look on, **consume to ashes**.

[*Loveless takes hold of her hand. Berinthia, breaking free—*]

BERINTHIA: O Lord, let me go; 'tis the **plague**, and we shall all be **infected**.

[*Loveless catches her in his arms and kisses her.*]

LOVELESS: Then we'll **die** together, my charming angel!

This feverish tango finally comes to its heart-palpitating end. Fun Stuff! If the actors follow the "choreography" of the lines, the dance is dynamic, precise, entertaining, marvelously alive. Indeed, the Restoration period, roughly 1660–1700, celebrated aliveness on stage. After a decade of sober humorless rule under the Puritan Commonwealth, which saw the closing of London's amoral theater houses, the English stage was *restored*, along with the monarchy. Vitality on the English stage was restored: For the first time in English history, women would step onto the stage, playing opposite men. This ignited a titillating dynamic, and playwrights fueled this dynamic by writing scenes laced with romantic tension and simmering sexuality. Metaphors provided a kind of sophisticated code by which men and women could flirt, be suggestive, and engage in bawdy innuendo.

Restoration drama was not the first of course to deploy extended metaphor within dialogue, but it was perhaps unprecedented in its daring unapologetic display of verbal tango, requiring outrageous new steps on the part of actors. This is one of the reasons why contemporary actors are so baffled and stymied by plays of this kind. They look *beneath* the language and, in doing so, miss the dance steps, the treasure glittering on the *surface*.

In our previous examples, the language of transference has been *direct*, in that the connection has been implicitly understood, taken for granted. For a more overt display of comparison, we have to glide our magical carpet to a special destination, one where the signposts are explicit and proud of it.

Chapter Four

SIMILE
This is like That

A simile is a specialized form or subspecies of metaphor. Similes also make connections, but they openly announce or display the connective tissue. Deriving from the Latin word for "like," a **Simile** (SI ma lee) *explicitly compares two elements not normally associated with one another, building an overt bridge between them by using "like" or "as" in the comparison.* While traditional metaphors "hide" the bridge between the two compared elements, similes show it off, reveling in the connection. A metaphor may state or imply that life is a battle, whereas a simile states that life is *like* a battle.

Similes derive their power from their explicitly declared links, the concrete and symmetrical way they set up correspondences between two elements. The listener is pointedly asked to entertain the notion that one element (source) is like another dissimilar element (vehicle) as a way of re-envisioning the former, giving it new resonance and meaning. "Look at how I've put together the world!" the speaker says to the listener. "I see a crazy link between these two things—check it out!" In Eric Overmyer's homage to the detective genre *In a Pig's Valise*, the gumshoe James Taxi describes an exotic young Latina nightclub singer as "hovering in the vicinity like heat on a desert highway." This shimmering connection grabs us, makes us smile, gives us a different take on the world.

Actors can relish and take full advantage of similes on the stage. Similes are not frivolous roadside ornaments, to be driven by on your way to somewhere else. They are vehicles to the destination. The connections they make are the very essence of the communication.

Homeric Simile: Setup and Payoff

Similes come in various guises or formulas. Many of these formulas follow a setup and payoff structure. The setup usually introduces the vehicle, brimming with fascinating attributes, and the payoff brings us back to the source—the original idea to which attributes are ascribed. In essence, the actor is asked to link the two parts—vocally—by finding the correspondences and

MAKING CONNECTIONS: Metaphor

highlighting them. Setup and Payoff. To understand this pattern, we can go to the earliest known origins of narrative simile, to the deepest wellsprings of Western storytelling—Homer's epic tales. The patterns of simile established in these works would be replicated by playwrights for the next 2,500 years. Actors were trained to identify and appreciate these structures—and to use them in performance.

If you pick up the *Iliad* or the *Odyssey*, you will be struck by the author's constant use of analogies. In the middle of a gripping battle sequence or in the wild throes of danger, the speaker will suddenly unfurl a lengthy simile that strives to sharpen a piece of detail or action. It's almost as if the story is momentarily suspended in time, so that the performer can bolster some image or idea by reaching for a riveting connection, one that surprises us and injects new perspective. Almost every page features this strategy. One of the more riveting—and violent—connections in the *Iliad* occurs when the Greek warrior Patroclus attacks the Trojan soldier Thestor, who is cowering in his chariot, paralyzed with fear.

> Patroclus rising beside him stabbed his right jawbone,
> ramming the spearhead square between his teeth so hard
> he hooked him by that spearhead over the chariot-rail,
> hoisted, dragged the Trojan out as an angler perched
> on a jutting rock ledge drags some fish from the sea,
> some noble catch, with line and glittering bronze hook.
> So with the spear Patroclus gaffed him off his car [*chariot*],
> his mouth gaping round the glittering point
> and flipped him down facefirst,
> dead as he fell, his breath blown away.
> (Book 16, 479–489, trans. by Robert Fagles)

In a rather remarkable, striking image, Thestor is explicitly compared to a hooked fish dragged from the sea, mouth gaping, barb embedded in its mouth. The listener's mind moves, with lightning speed, between the soldier on the battlefield and a fish in the sea—and compares the two. More specifically, this simile establishes an **AS/SO** structure. The **AS** contains the **setup**, while the **SO** brings in the **payoff**. This AS/SO structure is preceded by a specific *action* that draws the simile into play:

Chapter Four

action   he hooked him by that spearhead over the chariot-rail, hoisted, dragged the Trojan out

setup   AS an angler perched on a jutting rock ledge drags some fish from the sea, some noble catch, with line and glittering bronze hook.

payoff   SO with the spear Patroclus gaffed him off his car, his mouth gaping round the glittering point and flipped him down facefirst.

This structure provides valuable clues for the actor in performance. First, the performer must understand how the simile is launched by a specific piece of action—the spearing and hoisting of Thestor over the chariot rail. This action ignites the simile, beginning with the word "as." *A change in vocal melody and actor intention is required as the performer begins the setup portion of the simile.* We are no longer in the midst of battle, we are in the midst of a time-suspended comparison. We are no longer in the key of Action, we are in the key of Simile. The actor's *intention* is to make the connection to an out-of-action image very clear and arresting. Because the simile is not part of the literal action, it requires a change in:

◊ **Pitch**
◊ **Rhythm**
◊ **Stress**
◊ **Actor Intention**

The setup is signaled with this change. The setup has its own distinct rhythm and melody, which is then vocally differentiated or "stretched away" from the payoff, beginning with "so." The setup takes us into the connection or comparison, and the payoff brings us back to the thing being compared. We go up the hill, and then we slide back down the other side. The actor's voice can show us the explicit correspondence between the two halves of the simile:

MAKING CONNECTIONS: Metaphor

AS fisherman hooks squirming fish and yanks it out of the sea

SO Patroclus speared Thestor and flipped him facefirst
onto the ground.

This is *like* that, the actor says to her listener. The bridge between "this" and "that" must be clear and striking. The listener should not have to struggle to follow this connection, to cross the bridge. The power of simile is in asking the listener to make eye-opening connections and to imagine two odd bedfellows side by side. When this process is blurred, made inarticulate, difficult to follow, the audience checks out, begins to believe that the language of theater is somehow too heady, too far out, only for those select few (with Ph.D.s in Comparative Lit) to enjoy. It's not what Shakespeare believed or practiced, nor did his raucous ale-guzzling blue-collar crowd swarming into the Globe believe such things. They got language hot off the plate, sizzling with connections.

When the young Richard, later to become Richard III, ponders the difficulty in attaining the throne in Shakespeare's *Henry VI, Part 3*, he reaches for a Homeric simile to describe his intense longing for supreme power—and the seeming hopelessness of his ambition. Between him and the throne sit three older brothers and their potential offspring, all impediments to his ravenous desire.

> Why then I do but dream on sovereignty;
> Like one that stands upon a promontory [*cliff*]
> And spies a far-off shore where he would tread,
> Wishing his foot were equal with his eye;
> And chides the sea that sunders him from thence,
> Saying he'll lade [*drain*] it dry to have his way:
> So do I wish the crown, being so far off;
> And so I chide the means that keeps me from it.
> (3.2)

Richard, with his active searching mind, appreciates a good simile, and his follows the setup and payoff formula, using LIKE/SO in this case. He cues the simile with an action statement:

Chapter Four

Why then I do but dream on sovereignty

Simply dreaming about sovereignty, the crown, does not adequately describe his experience. He wants us to receive a much more electric view of this desire, this dreaming. And so he hooks into a little fable about a man standing on an ocean cliff looking way out across the water to a piece of shoreline, an island, in the vast distance. That's when the simile kicks in, beginning with "like":

setup   LIKE one who stands upon a promontory
And spies a far-off shore where he would tread,
Wishing his foot were equal with his eye;
And chides the sea, that sunders him from thence,
Saying he'll lade [*drain*] it dry to have his way:

payoff   SO do I wish the crown, being so far off;
And so I chide the means that keeps me from it.

The man wishes "his foot were equal with his eye," wishes he was instantly standing on that distant shore. But how to get there? He will drain the water between cliff and shore. Then he finally brings the comparison "back home" in the payoff section, directly linking the attributes of sea and shore to his quest for the throne. It may be useful to recite a very simple version:

LIKE a man who sees far-off shoreline, craves to be there, wants to drain the water between him and shore

SO I do wish the crown, equally far off, and so I rail at the obstacles that stand between me and it.

Technically, there are two key aspects to making the Setup/Payoff structure clear and vivid in the actor's speaking:

Make the setup (vehicle) vocally distinct from the payoff (source).

MAKING CONNECTIONS: Metaphor

The vehicle provides the movement, as it takes the listener to some exotic fascinating locale. It is the basis for the comparison, featuring bold sparks of connection, so it must be differentiated from the source. That is, it requires its own pitch, stress, and rhythm. The audience has to know when the comparison is brought "back home," so the actor vocally guides the listener across the bridge from setup to payoff. The vehicle, the man and the sea, provides attributes to the source—Richard and the crown. The vehicle is *distinct* from the source, though they are linked:

> **Find the correspondences—and let them call and respond to each other across the bridge.**

In Richard's speech, the correspondences are clear:

> **Richard = man standing on cliff (promontory)**
>
> **far-off shore = crown**
>
> **sea = obstacles**
>
> **chides the sea = chide the means (i.e., brothers)**

Man desiring distant shore is like Richard thirsting for distant crown. **This is like *that*.** These words call and respond to each other, vocally. Equally important, the intention to make this clear must be burning in the actor's imagination.

Put another way, the simile is not some vague comparison that the actor—or audience—can choose to ignore. It is the very stuff of Richard's mind. It's how he thinks—in extravagant dramatic outlandish ways. He wants us to see his seething mind, his hunger for power, his thirst for the crown, so he creates a fable, a connection to something rather unusual, an image we can grasp and perhaps relate to. Good theater, like good art, wants us to relate to something. This is *like* that, Richard says to us. Do you follow me? Do you understand me? Are you with me?

"Are you with me?" This is a question every actor can ask of the listener. If the listener is not with you, or is only partially with you, it's time to regroup and reach for a more vivid mode of communication, one that makes greater demands on both actor and audience. If you are playing Proteus in

Chapter Four

Two Gentlemen of Verona, you want the listener to fully grasp—and savor—the eccentric comparisons you create. In a heartbeat, the fickle Proteus has suddenly fallen out of love with Julia and in love with Silvia, his best friend's girl. He describes this romantic reversal by drawing a comparison.

> Even as one heat another heat expels,
> Or as one nail by strength drives out another,
> So the remembrance of my former love
> Is by a newer object quite forgotten.
>
> (2.4)

Proteus plunges directly into the simile, without any preceding action statement. He gives us two distinct vehicles (AS), which are connected explicitly to the source (SO). In Elizabethan times, the application of external heat, like a hot compress, was thought to expel or ease the pain of a burn—another kind of heat. One heat replaces another heat. But Proteus is not completely satisfied with this analogy, so he offers another one: a new nail drives out an old nail. If you have ever wielded a hammer, you will recall the way you place a strong new nail under the flank of an embedded rusty nail—and pound it out of its entrenched position. What an image! Especially when it is linked to one person displacing another! Proteus then takes us across the bridge into the Payoff: **SO** the memory of his "former love" is now erased by a "newer object." We can strip it down to its bare bones, paraphrasing it:

> As one heat is expelled by a stronger heat
> Or as one nail pounds out another nail
> So Julia is driven out by Silvia.

"Look at how I've put together the world!" Proteus tells us. "This is how I see my predicament." He wants us to make a connection between two dissimilar things. He wants us to imagine it, to enjoy it, to think about it. The actor has to have this same fervent desire. The simile is not a piece of text to be tossed aside as the actor sprints toward the tape of linear dialogue down the road. Do you see how the setup/payoff structure guides the actor? Gives him clues for which words to emphasize or highlight? We can view the correspondences this way:

MAKING CONNECTIONS: Metaphor

Even as **one heat** *another heat* expels,
Or as **one nail** by strength drives out *another*,

So the remembrance of my **former love**
Is by a *newer object* quite forgotten.

Make the corresponding words talk to each other. That's the key. If you forget—or are intimidated by—all the other technical explanations of Homeric simile, remember that you are letting the linking words call and respond to one another. In the end, we arrive always at the simple, underlying premise:

This is like **That**

This amazingly simple statement undergirds Shakespeare's dialogue. It is one of the keys to grasping his use of language. His characters are always searching for the extraordinary connection. In doing so, they continue to stretch the boundary lines of the world and our interpretation of it. Each striking comparison opens a new window onto the world. Indeed, the use of analogy changes our understanding of an event or an emotion, as our brains swim between the source and the vehicle, sparking new outlooks, new thoughts, a new appreciation of something we had not thought about in quite that way before. The world we thought we knew is suddenly tilted ten degrees—as we adjust our lens to a new way of seeing.

Punchline Similes

Many similes are also fun and playful. They worship wit and anticipation. They idolize delight and a humorous take on the world. This kind of simile often falls into a setup-and-punchline format, without the AS/SO structure featured in Homeric similes. And they are not so concerned with symmetrical correspondences. Instead, they tease us by building anticipation in the same way we await the answer to a riddle. "The stock market lately has acted like a happy drunk at a bar," says a keen investor. We lean forward, eager to hear the explanation or answer to this teaser. "He gets high, promises the moon, then falls off his stool, rebounds, makes new promises, falls." These similes throw interest forward in a sentence as we await the punchline. The more the

117

Chapter Four

actor is aware of the structure, the more he can exploit the punchline simile in performance.

In William Wycherley's *The Country Wife*, two gallants, Harcourt and Dorilant, are trading witty remarks about their favorite pastime—mistresses. The burning question of the moment: How much time should be allotted to their company? "A mistress should be like a little country retreat near the town," says Mr. Dorilant. That's the setup. It elicits a "How so?" from the listener because it needs further elaboration. The listener leans in, wanting to know more, as Dorilant uncorks the punchline: "—Not to dwell in constantly, but only for a night and away, to taste the town [*city*] better when a man returns."

> **setup** A mistress should be like a little country retreat near the town.
>
> **punchline** Not to dwell in constantly, but only for a night and away, to taste the town better when a man returns.

When we tell a joke or a riddle, our voice savors the clever punchline, gives it a distinct flavor, one different from the setup. The voice teases or provokes curiosity in the first half, then provides a check-out-this-wit drum roll in the second half.

In John Dryden's delicious Restoration romp *Marriage à la Mode*, Palamede asks his lady friend, Doralice, for a little "comfort" before his impending marriage (to another woman), which signals the end of his carefree adventurous bachelor life and thus represents, for Palamede, an approaching day of doom.

> A little comfort from a mistress before a man is going to give himself in marriage is as good as a lusty dose of strong water [*whiskey*] to a dying malefactor [*criminal sentenced to hang*]:
>
> it takes away the sense of hell and hanging from him.
>
> (5.1, bold mine)

MAKING CONNECTIONS: Metaphor

Palamede whets our appetite with his setup and then uncorks a resounding punchline. By providing some "comfort," Doralice can take away his sense of "hell and hanging." Doralice responds with a wildly risqué metaphor, using money as transference for male sexual potency.

> No, good Palamede, I must not be so injurious to your bride.
> *'Tis ill drawing from the bank today when all your ready money is payable tomorrow.*

Even though she responds with an outright metaphor, Doralice still provides a kind of punchline or explanation to her thesis: "I must not be so injurious to your bride." The ensuing punchline takes us by surprise, provokes a bawdy response. Later in the scene, Doralice concludes that she and Palamede should maintain their strong attraction for one another by never consummating their relationship; she showcases her own punchline simile to sharpen this idea.

> The only way to keep us new to one another is never to enjoy, as they keep grapes by hanging them upon a line:
> *they must touch nothing if you would preserve them fresh.*

"But then they wither and grow dry in the very keeping," Palamede complains, but to no avail! Again, Doralice's simile invites the actor to slice away the punchline from the setup, to give each half its own distinct ***phrasing*** and ***melody***. Imagine a comedian who spoke everything in a flat monotone, who made no distinctions between setup and punchline, between one joke and another. Great stand-up comics know how to keep our listening alive, how to continually re-energize our hearing. They mix it up vocally, take us up, down, and around the loop. They want their audience leaning in, ready to rumble, eager to follow the Pied Piper along the road. They don't want us to miss an important part of the setup because the success of the payoff depends on our ability to follow each detail of the story. Indeed, their livelihood depends on it. Actors can develop this same passion for—or commitment to—vocal dynamics and skill, knowing that the success of a performance is not only dependent on their "inner life" but on the mastery of rhetorical craft, which shapes our participation in the play.

Chapter Four

Showoff Similes

Ah, the showoff simile. This is probably the most prevalent and most popular form of the simile. Openly flashy one-liners that capture our attention and take us out of our ordinariness. "I was dizzier than a dose of peroxide and as feverish as a bottle of aspirin," says James Taxi, the detective hero of *In a Pig's Valise*. Showoff similes say something about the speaker as well as the subject of comparison. They reveal personality. The speaker delights in putting together two unexpected things or in finding an unusual connection. The showoff simile, really, is a celebration of language as well as the multicolored landscape of our world. Rather than shy away from the showoff simile, actors should get hip to its outlandishness.

Nowhere, perhaps, is the showoff simile more on display than in Eric Overmyer's *In a Pig's Valise*. A full-out celebration—and parody—of the 1940s Raymond Chandler detective genre, *In a Pig's Valise* unabashedly revels in detective lingo, in zany, corny, pretentious, outrageous, witty one-liners. It doesn't care about naturalistic dialogue or verisimilitude. This play is a verbal party and everyone is invited. Just bring a simile and you are in the door. A showoff simile, preferably. James Taxi establishes the style early as he stands at the corner of Neon and Lonely, late at night, in front of the Heartbreak Hotel.

> The air was like Liquid Paper. Whoo. My chronic hypothermia was coming on like a hit of purple haze. Cold cojones, pal. I was shaking like a maracas player on the Feast Day of St. Zenophobe of the Green Card. I played a round of pocket pool and kept hanging in. The fog continued to ladle itself on. Like pea soup in a Merchant Marine mess hall. Like interest on an easy-payment credit plan. Like suffering similes in exhausted sub-genres of pop-tic and modern lit. You couldn't hack through it with an M-16....The kiss-me-Wednesday night air was putting a chill on my bones like jelly on a gefilte fish.
>
> (Act 1)

What the actor needs here is not so much a specific technique or tool but a dose of courage. Bravery. Many performers tend to apologize for this kind of

MAKING CONNECTIONS: Metaphor

language and undersell it. They get queasy standing out on the ledge of verbalmania, so they speak the dialogue in a less than inspired way. Meekly, without soul. But James Taxi is proud of his whacky comparisons. He wants the listener to notice them, one way or another. Each successive simile climbs further up the mountain of verbal delight. The listener can laugh, frown, think the verbiage pretentious or corny—or brilliant, but the listener must be engaged. That's critical. This language grabs the listener, says, "Alright, who wants to play? Check out this crazy stuff and let's rock the genre, baby." This text needs an actor who can play at that level. It needs an actor who can step into the outrageousness of this world, take a drag on that cigarette, adjust his fedora, and let fly the words.

When Taxi meets the heroine, the mysterious Dolores Con Leche, a nightclub entertainer, he feels the chemistry between them. Dolores is a gal who can trade similes with him.

> TAXI: I feel like a side o' slaw strewn across a soggy paper plate.
> DOLORES: Those hard-boiled similes get pretty thin. As thin as the skin on a cup of cocoa.
> TAXI: As thin as the crust on an East Coast pizza pie.

After a great adventure together, laced with clever verbal repartee, our two heroes enjoy a final intimate moment at the end of the play. Dolores grabs Taxi, bends him into a tango swoon, and gives him a long rough kiss. In the middle of this moment, Taxi suddenly breaks off.

> TAXI (*In the VO*): She had lips as sweet and full as ten pounds of sucre in a five-pound sack. They turned my spine to flan....
> (*Dolores drops him on the floor.*)
> DOLORES: You gotta see somebody about that. I'm not spending the weekend with somebody who talks to himself in the past tense.
> TAXI: Promise.
> (*He picks himself up. They lock eyes and get steamy.*)
> DOLORES: I don't care what they say about you. I think you're muy picante.
> TAXI: What exactly do they say about me?

Chapter Four

> DOLORES: That you're fast as a claims settlement.
> TAXI: Irony. I like that in a woman. You know, Con Leche, you're about as subtle as a pitcher of sangria.
> DOLORES: Tell me more, big fella.
> TAXI: You come on strong, like you're a double shot of tequila with a brew back. But you're really about as tough to take as a spring day.
> DOLORES: Sweet. You hard-boiled guys have maple syrup in your veins.
> TAXI: Don't stop now.
> DOLORES: Taxi, you come on like a mouthful of razor blades, but you're really as hard-edged as a flour tortilla. You're as sweet as sopapilla.
> TAXI: I've swapped similes with saps from Sunset to Sepulveda, but sister, you're something special.
> (Act 2)

As the preacher said to the parishioners, "You gotta believe." Dialogue like this requires a leap of faith. Once the actor takes that leap, she finds herself in a brave new world, where style, genre, and words are shaping character, motive, and the play. She finds herself in a theatrical funhouse, where the peculiarities of our world are celebrated and enjoyed. If the performer leads the way, takes bold steps into this funhouse, the audience will follow.

TAKING STOCK

When the world closes in on us, gets monotonous and predictable, we reach for metaphor to open it up by revealing new, previously unexamined connections. These connections propel imaginative movement, as the listener's mind travels from **this** to **that—and compares the two in a flash**. Metaphorical runs, verbal tango, and Homeric similes are all devoted to lifting us out of our habitual watering holes and taking us to brave and rowdy new places. Once the actor sees the power and creative force of metaphor, he transforms his approach to the dialogue of *transference*. Instead of bypassing it, seeing it

MAKING CONNECTIONS: Metaphor

as a superfluous detour, she takes advantage of metaphor's ability to re-create the world by vocally highlighting a "run" across several lines or by accepting the invitation to "dance" with a scene partner—as they share a comparison, passing it back and forth through vocal interplay. Suddenly, the actor finds wit, play, fable-like stories, and luminous new perspectives in the connection between *this* and *that*. The actor unleashes an electric communication that captivates the listener, surrounds him with exciting images and delightful surprises. "Watch how this idea is reassembled in a bold new package!" the actor tells the listener.

The metaphor engages the human mind in a profoundly different way than the linear phrase. Actors should be aware of this distinction. It will keep their radars attuned to the connections featured in verbally adventurous plays—and to the changes in speaking that they require.

Our fantastical flying carpet awaits your pleasure. If you find a connection, it will take you there. Making connections is the magic of metaphor.

Chapter Five

MANTRAS, SPELLS, AND GROOVES: Repetition

Over 200,000 pilgrims flocked to the nation's capital on that historic day. They had traveled from every state, by bus and truck and train and foot. They had answered the call to participate in the March on Washington for Civil Rights, then the largest demonstration of its kind in the history of the United States. Two hundred thousand sojourners stood in the sweltering August heat of 1963, between the Washington Monument and the Lincoln Memorial, to share a vision of an America that honors its promise of liberty and justice for all. They had come to hear and feel the words that would describe their struggle and inspire their hope. The keynote speaker on that day was the Reverend Martin Luther King, Jr., a Black Baptist minister and civil rights leader who had sprung to national prominence leading the Montgomery Bus Boycott seven years earlier. The crowd surged forward as King stepped onto the podium, before the stone memorial to Abraham Lincoln.

King started his speech by noting that, one hundred years after the signing of the Emancipation Proclamation, the African American—the "Negro"— was still not free. He painted a picture of the Black American living on "an island of poverty in the vast ocean of material prosperity." The Negro, he argued, was an exile in his own land, banished to the unlit corners of American society. The audience moved in closer, vocally responding to King's oratory. America, King continued, had defaulted on its promissory note of equal opportunity and justice. He spoke of the urgency of the moment, of racial harmony, of nonviolence, of moral battle and vigor.

—And then Martin Luther King, imploring his listeners to resist the pull of despair, calmly looked out across the surging crowd...

I still have a dream. It is a dream deeply rooted in the American dream. *I have a dream* that one day this nation will rise up and

MANTRAS, SPELLS, AND GROOVES: Repetition

live out the true meaning of its creed—"we hold these truths to be self-evident, that all men are created equal."

King, drawing on his decade of speeches delivered in the trenches of struggle and at church pulpits, continued.

> *I have a dream* that one day on the red hills of Georgia, sons of former slaves and sons of former slave-owners will be able to sit down together at the table of brotherhood...

> *I have a dream* that my four little children will one day live in a nation where they will not be judged by the color of their skin but by the content of their character. *I have a dream today!*

(bold italics mine)

I have a dream....I have a dream....I have a dream.... King's voice soared across the National Mall. He would continue to repeat the phrase in the remaining section of the speech. He had used this phrase in a little-known earlier speech but suddenly felt the spontaneous impulse to release it on this Grand Stage. His instincts were right. This phrase changed American history on that day and embedded itself into the consciousness of the 200,000 gathered there, as well as the millions who were watching on television. The seventeen-minute speech, perhaps the most important in the American 20th century, became known as the "I have a dream" speech overnight. President John F. Kennedy, greeting King at the White House immediately after the speech, extended his hand with the welcoming words: "I have a dream."

If King had used the phrase "I have a dream" only once during the speech, would he have generated the same impact with his address? Would anyone refer to the speech as the "I have a dream" speech today? What happened that day? What were the effects of King's words? King's speech, like every great speech, was a performance and, as such, can be examined by today's stage actor to see what lessons it may yield. King expressed a profound message, yes, but he also found a verbal package—and *voice*—that gave it everlasting appeal. In particular, he featured the strategy of repetition.

Chapter Five

What is the power of repetition? What is gained when the speaker repeats something? The classical age knew the secrets of repetition and trained young speakers to take advantage of them in persuading an audience. Stirring religious oratory, which understood the effects of repetitive chants, was something King grew up listening to in the Black Baptist churches of the South. What did he learn there? What "lost knowledge" might the actor acquire today?

In earlier centuries, young performers were trained to recognize and use the rhetorical figures of Repetition. These figures were spread across several broad fronts:

◊ Repetition of Words and Phrases
◊ Repetition of Ideas
◊ Repetition of Structure, Sound

Let's take a look at each of these categories and examine the opportunities that present themselves to the actor in performance.

REPETITION OF WORDS AND PHRASES

EPIMONE
The Spellbinder

When a speaker *frequently repeats a phrase in order to emphasize a particular point*, he is employing **Epimone** (e PIM o nee). The repeated phrase arrives *after an interval*, like a refrain in a piece of music that reoccurs throughout the tune. The phrase, after a period of "tarry and delay"—the Greek meaning of epimone—comes back around the bend. Each time the phrase comes 'round the corner it increases its impact and appeal, as it stamps itself into our consciousness, engraining its message.

Earlier centuries knew that this kind of verbal structure had a special charm, a kind of magical *incantation* that listeners find irresistibly compelling and seductive. The mind begins to anticipate the arrival of the "refrain" and

MANTRAS, SPELLS, AND GROOVES: Repetition

falls into a kind of rhythmic groove, giving assent to the sentiment expressed. Epimone is persuasive. The speaker invites the listener into a spell, one that gathers sound, rhythm, and message into a unified repeating "chant." How can the actor use this spell in performance? Let's take a look at an example from Bernard Shaw's play *Getting Married*, where the battle of the sexes takes on unexpected twists and turns.

The experienced and captivating Mrs. George, oft-injured in the wars of love, falls into an otherworldly trance as she addresses her past lover (or lovers?), the man to whom she has given her heart.

> When you loved me I gave you the whole sun and stars to play with. I gave you eternity in a single moment, strength of the mountains in one clasp of your arms, and the volume of all the seas in one impulse of your soul. A moment only; but ***was it not enough?*** Were you not paid then for all the rest of your struggle on earth? Must I mend your clothes and sweep your floors as well? ***Was it not enough?*** I paid the price without bargaining: I bore the children without flinching: was that a reason for heaping fresh burdens on me? I carried the child in my arms: must I carry the father too? When I opened the gates of paradise, were you blind? was it nothing to you? When all the stars sang in your ears and all the winds swept you into the heart of heaven, were you deaf? were you dull? was I no more to you than a bone to a dog? ***Was it not enough?*** We spent eternity together; and you ask me for a little lifetime more. We possessed all the universe together; and you ask me to give you my scanty wages as well. I have given you the greatest of all things; and you ask me to give you little things. I gave you your own soul: you ask me for my body as a plaything. ***Was it not enough? Was it not enough?***
>
> (bold italics mine)

Compulsive antithesis and epimone power this fascinating speech. Like a haunting refrain, "Was it not enough?" echoes throughout the speech, in this case at rather unpredictable intervals. Her main point: "What more could I have given? Did I not give everything of myself? And yet you kept demanding more and more." With each repetition of "Was it not enough?" the speaker

Chapter Five

turns the screw yet tighter, gives the phrase more resonance and indignation. In performance, the actor can exploit this repeating figure in two fundamental ways:

> ✔ **Vary it** ("You Can't Go Home Again")
> ✔ **Justify it** (Why did you say it again?)

The question "Was it not enough?" cannot gather force and persuasion if it stays vocally monotonous and does not exploit or justify its repetitive structure. The first time we hear the phrase, we do not know that it will be repeated later. The first speaking of the phrase establishes a benchmark. It gets the listener's attention. The second speaking builds or riffs off the first—and continues to grow dynamically throughout the speech. The change may be subtle or it may be more dramatic. The actor has freedom to experiment. But there must be *some change*, a reason you call on the phrase again…and again.

> **When we repeat something, we are saying to the listener that the phrase is supervital, worthy of his continued examination and reflection.**

The voice naturally follows this logic by finding ways to justify the phrase and continually reenergize the listener's ear. Not in an arbitrary way, or in a purely technical way, but in a way where the voice is mirroring the increasing urgency of the message. In King's "I have a dream" speech, he modulates his voice, raising his pitch, increasingly accenting—and often lengthening—his key phrase with each repeating cycle. "Look at my vision, do you see it yet? here it comes again, look at it again, do you see the dream yet? who among you is with me?" The dream builds, it grows, it does not look back or stay "at home." Likewise, with Mrs. George, she is not content with a one-time utterance of her point. Her point thrives on repetition; indeed, it *needs* the repetition to detonate its full value.

We can attempt to illustrate this *need* by looking at one interpretation (among a million) that uses the gathering spell of epimone:

> Was it not enough?...
> **Was it not enough?...**

MANTRAS, SPELLS, AND GROOVES: Repetition

Was it not ENOUGH?...
Was—it—not—enough? WAS IT NOT ENOUGH?

With each repeating phrase, the speaker's sense of injustice grows and gathers force, the sense of being brazenly taken for granted, of giving and giving and not receiving acknowledgment, of emotional investment not reciprocated, of being asked for more and more and more...

Play with this speech and discover the many ways you can hook into the mysterious appeal of epimone. Experiment with the repeating question. Might there be an interpretation that decreases in intensity with each repetition? What effect does that create in the listener? Here's a bold little experiment: Try omitting all of the "Was it not enough?" questions from the speech—and see what, if anything, the speech loses in its impact. Or, what if you keep the first question but cut all the rest. Have you lost anything? That's the test. Put another way, what does the performer *gain* with the repetitive strategy?

Let's try another experiment. What happens when you make no adjustment, either intention-wise or vocally, in the repetitive structure?

Was it not enough?...
Was it not enough?...
Was it not enough?...
Was it not enough?   Was it not enough?

This may be hard to do, for the figure of epimone really craves dynamism. It wants the performer to ride its gathering wave, to take advantage of its theatrical power. When there is no justification or need for the repetition, epimone cannot awaken. Dullness and casual risk-free talk cannot activate the spell of Mrs. George's message.

Spellbinding Uses

Rhetorical figures, like epimone, can also be put to more nefarious ends. In Milton's *Paradise Lost*, the Narrator describes the Serpent as pouring suggestive words into the ear of a sleeping Eve, giving rise to strange new desires

Chapter Five

and dangerous curiosity. In Shakespeare's *Othello*, Iago is a master of suggestive language, dripping sly insinuations into the ears of his listeners. His treacherous use of epimone is a case in point. Speaking to the gullible Roderigo, whom he needs to employ as an unwitting agent of his poisonous plot against Othello the Moor, Iago attempts to convince the disconsolate gentleman that his secret and pining love for Desdemona will one day be requited, that he should not give up hope. Desdemona will eventually sever her marriage ties with Othello, claims Iago. Roderigo, therefore, must shake off his blues and prepare himself; he must get ready for that glorious day. Listen to how Iago weaves an infectious spell of epimone to rejuvenate the depressed Roderigo.

> I could never better stead thee than now. **Put money in thy purse**; follow thou the wars; defeat thy favor with an usurp'd beard. I say **put money in thy purse**. It cannot be that Desdemona should long continue her love to the Moor—**put money in thy purse**—nor he his to her. It was a violent commencement in her, and thou shalt see an answerable sequestration—**put but money in thy purse**. These Moors are changeable in their wills—**fill thy purse with money**. The food that to him now is as luscious as locusts [*sweet fruit of the carob tree*], shall be to him shortly as bitter as the coloquintida [*sour apple*]. She must change for youth; when she is sated with his body, she will find the error of her choice. She must have change, she must; therefore **put money in thy purse**....If sanctimony and a frail vow betwixt an erring barbarian and a super-subtle Venetian be not too hard for my wits and all the tribe of hell, thou shalt enjoy her. Therefore **make money**.
> (1.3, bold italics mine)

After urging the young Roderigo to grow a soldier-like beard, Iago turns to an assessment of the relationship between Othello and Desdemona. The same "violent commencement" or brash decision that made Desdemona marry Othello will receive an "answerable sequestration" or equally abrupt ending, predicts Iago. Likewise, Othello is changeable in his lust ("will"): he will soon surfeit on the sweet fruit of Desdemona, finding bitterness in its aftertaste. Besides, Othello is too old for the passionately youthful Desdemona. She will no doubt crave change, Iago insists. This weak and

MANTRAS, SPELLS, AND GROOVES: Repetition

ill-matched marriage vow between a roving barbarian and a refined Venetian woman will not endure.

Interwoven among these predictions is the key repeating phrase: ***Put money in thy purse*** or slight variations of it. What to make of this phrase? While its specific meaning is open to varying interpretations, it seems clear—in this context—that the phrase draws upon a punchy maxim, one that inspires boundless confidence, shining hope, and bursting optimism.

You can bet on it!
You'll hit the jackpot!
Never give up hope!
Go for it!

It also may be interesting to note that money was often equated with male sexual potency in Shakespeare's time as well as in the English Restoration period. Roderigo will soon be spending money. Iago may be preparing Roderigo for his sexual enjoyment ("thou shalt enjoy her") of Desdemona. Be that as it may, Iago's refrain serves to bolster and rev up the sagging spirits of Roderigo.

Listen to how Iago slips his refrain into Roderigo's ear in a *variety of ways*. Sometimes the phrase is lit up in bold neon, as in his first utterance, which establishes a starting point. At other times, the phrase is almost subliminally (if we can borrow a term from modern psychology) dropped into Roderigo's consciousness:

> It cannot be that Desdemona should long continue her love to the Moor—*put money in thy purse*—nor he his to her.

Iago almost whispers the phrase, like the Serpent to the sleeping Eve. He sneaks it in as an aside, nonchalantly, quickly, without fanfare. The phrase, Iago knows, will work its magic, coiling itself around the mind of Roderigo. Each time the phrase comes around, it provides an energizing **jolt**, a **spur**, a psychological **push**—and that is an action that the actor can play. That is one of the ways that epimone works its charm. Iago, like a wizard-musician, plays his refrain with a variety of dynamics, each time jolting Roderigo into higher levels of optimism and allowing him to see that the dream of Desdemona is becoming clearer, more attainable, within his sensual grasp:

131

Chapter Five

Put money in thy purse
Put money in thy purse
—PUT MONEY IN THY PURSE—
Put but money in thy purse
Fill-thy-purse-with-money

Again, these are not random changes, but ones that Iago needs in order to keep refreshing his point, as he plays them with a variety of notes. In addition to using melodic variations, Iago works his speech rhythmically, the refrain serving to punctuate and at times syncopate the tempo. For the spell to work, the actor must keep the repeating phrase alive and new and exciting. Monotony and verbal apathy will break the spell. After the pep talk with Iago, Roderigo has a new spring in his step, buoyed by new hope: "I am chang'd," he happily declares. "I will sell all my land," he announces, responding to Iago's dictum. He waltzes off, with visions of a beckoning Desdemona swirling before him.

In Suzan-Lori Parks' Pulitzer Prize–winning play *Topdog/Underdog*, two African American brothers, ironically named Lincoln and Booth, attempt to find redemption against the background of a fractured family history. Lincoln strives to piece together the fragments of his childhood, seized by the painful remembrance of the daily battles endured by "moms" and "pops."

> Each of them had a special something that they was struggling against. Moms had hers. Pops had his. And they was struggling. We moved out of that nasty apartment into a house. A whole house. It wernt perfect but it was a house and theyd bought it and they brought us there and everything we owned, figuring we could be a family in that house and them things, them two separate things each of them was struggling against, would just leave them be. Them things would see thuh house and be impressed and just leave them be. Would see thuh job Pops had and how he shined his shoes every night before he went to bed, shining them shoes whether they needed it or not, and thuh thing he was struggling against would see all that and just let him be, and thuh thing Moms was struggling against, it would see the food on the table every night and listen to her voice when she'd read to us sometimes, the

MANTRAS, SPELLS, AND GROOVES: Repetition

clean clothes, the buttons sewed on all right and it would just let her be. Just let us all be, just regular people living in a house.
(Scene 5)

Struggle is a haunting refrain in this speech, gathering force with each successive repetition. Lincoln keeps coming back to a variation of the phrase, "and they was struggling," hoping to find a redemptive mystery or catharsis within its sound and meaning. He *needs* each variation, as his life has been defined by struggle and a desperate attempt to understand its origins. For the actor, each refrain can build upon—and echo—the previous one, as Lincoln unpeels layers of memory, getting closer to the lived experience of his parents.

Epimone then is a spellbinder. It can lift the human spirit, reinforce a compulsive thought, or it can envelop one in layers of deceit. Epimone brings a crescendo of emphasis, strengthening a point with each cycle of the carousel. In each instance, the repetitive chant fuels the message's power and charm. For epimone to affect the listener, it must be exploited by the speaker, the actor. Like a preacher ablaze with a message, the actor must unleash the dynamics of voice, stand bravely at the pulpit, and find intoxicating new justification for the continued use of the refrain. The human mind is inexplicably riveted by the strategy of epimone—and the recognition of this fact, alone, can forever alter the performer's appreciation for the possibilities that this cyclical figure presents.

PALILOGIA
The Reinforcer

The harried mom, scurrying about the kitchen, suddenly catches sight of Junior reaching for the lit front burner.
  Don't touch that stove! she blurts in a panic. Junior's hand freezes in midair, looks perplexedly at his mother, who, with resolute purpose, looking him directly in the eye, repeats the phrase, this time driving home the point with a very deliberate, cadenced urgency:

Don't—touch—that—stove.

Chapter Five

Junior slowly lowers his hand, backs away from the stove, smiles sheepishly at his relieved mom. The first statement caught his attention, but the second triggered action. It provided a strong reinforcement of the first.

Think how often we feel the urge to reinforce an idea or a command by repeating it—immediately—a second time, often with increased vehemence. A one-time utterance is not enough; we feel an overwhelming need to hammer the phrase again, accenting a new urgency of meaning. When the *speaker repeats a phrase or word—back-to-back—she is employing the rhetorical strategy of* **Palilogia** (pa li LO jee a), a Greek word meaning "recapitulation." The word or phrase is recapitulated, immediately repeated, without the strategy of delay that is the characteristic of epimone. Palilogia offers today's performer a blast of **vehemence** or **sharpened emphasis**. It broadcasts a wake-up signal to the listener and, as such, is a key tool of communication on stage.

Suzan-Lori Parks peppers her contemporary plays with this emphatic figure. In *Topdog/Underdog*, Booth and Lincoln, two brothers, punch each other with palilogia, bolstering their points, slashing each other with repetitive razor-sharp verbal jabs. Booth wants to team up with his older brother Lincoln on a money-making scam called the three-card monte. Lincoln, Booth notes, was the best card-throwing hustler on the street. But Lincoln refuses to reignite his con artist past: "I don't touch the cards, 3-Card. I don't touch the cards no more." Booth, who needs his brother's superior card-throwing skills and savvy, sees his "economic opportunity" crumble and desperately rips into his brother.

> Here I am trying to earn a living and you standing in my way. YOU STANDING IN MY WAY, LINK!
>
> (Scene 1)

Parks leaves little doubt about how the figure of palilogia plays out here. Her capital letters convey a ratcheting up of vehemence. They are a neon-lit clue for the performer. The actor must make an adjustment between the first and second use of the phrase, "You standing in my way." The second phrase must build on—or respond to—the first phrase in some way. That is the crucial point. The two phrases cannot be identical in delivery if the power of palilogia is to be released. And yet many actors, surprisingly, do

MANTRAS, SPELLS, AND GROOVES: Repetition

not take advantage of this figure and simply repeat the phrase without any particular distinction. In this case, the second phrase can be theoretically cut from the text since it does little to add or bolster or reinforce the first utterance. But palilogia wants the performer to drive in that nail with vigorous swings:

    a-b-c-d   **A-B-C-D!**

While palilogia may often feature a stronger attack on the second phrase, it does not always subscribe to this strategy. Sometimes, the repeated phrase can be explored in a variety of dynamics, particularly when the surrounding context carries a more mysterious, open-ended invitation. As Othello, torch in hand, enters Desdemona's bedroom, he watches her sleep, steeling himself for the murder he is about to commit.

> *It is the cause, it is the cause*, my soul;
> Let me not name it to you, you chaste stars,
> *It is the cause.*
>
>   (5.1, italics mine)

Othello focuses on "*the cause*," Desdemona's supposed **crime** (of adulterous betrayal), rather than on the "criminal"—Desdemona. His repetitive phrase emphasizes the crime, the crime, rather than his own wife. In this way, Othello can try to distance himself from the horrific event by casting himself as an obedient officer of justice, rather than as a man personally avenging a wrong. Here, palilogia works as a kind of placating balm for Othello's poisoned mind, giving him desperate reassurance that his impending action is defensible—and justifiable:

    it is the *cause*
    it is the *cause*

There are of course an infinity of ways the actor can play with this particular example. But the second phrase must play off the first—in some way—in order for the emphasis to take hold. Othello *needs* this repeating figure to reinforce his resolve, to fortify his determination. After a brief interval, with a hint of epimone, he repeats the key phrase a third time:

135

Chapter Five

It is the cause.

With each repetition, Othello gains resolve and emotional detachment, a way for him to proceed into the dark night of his deed. He needs the reinforcement of palilogia to clarify his clinical motives and to banish competing voices of guilt or repentance or sorrow. Othello cannot let his thoughts sink into the deep waters of repentance, so he attempts to fix his mind on his judicial task: "Yet she must die, or else she'll betray more men." To steel himself, he reaches for the whip of palilogia.

EPIZEUXIS
The Mantra

When palilogia reaches a compulsive gallop of repetition, it turns the reins over to its younger wild-eyed cousin, Epizeuxis, who drives the horses with increasing fury. **Epizeuxis** (e pi ZOOK sis), a "fastening together," *gathers emphatic power by continually repeating a word or phrase, in a mantra of obsession.* Epizeuxis is palilogia on overdrive. Rather than the compressed one-two punch of palilogia, epizeuxis relies on bombardment. It reveals a character on the edge, an obsession with a concept or feeling that can only be released—or explored—through compulsive repetition.

In Tony Kushner's *Slavs!*, Popolitipov, a Soviet apparatchik in his sour sixties, lays bare his feelings to Katherina, a dissatisfied young woman who works as a security guard and who views him with a mixture of disdain and repulsive bemusement. Still, the two share cigarettes and vodka together. On this particular occasion, an emotional Popolitipov takes a swig and pleads his case.

> That night, that night, when I saw you that night, I was walking in the Arbat, you had fallen in the snow, sleeping in the gutter, dirty, drunk, rude, radiant: I was overwhelmed with lust, and then followed—love. Love. Love. Love. Love. Even in a corrupt and loveless world, love can be born.

> (2.1)

MANTRAS, SPELLS, AND GROOVES: Repetition

Notice that the speech begins with a dose of palilogia, as Popolitipov stresses the importance of "that night, that night," his first encounter with Katherina. He goes on to reveal the feelings she evoked in him on that fateful night, how he discovered the rapturous stirrings of love. He cannot get enough of this word, love, as he repeats it five times in a row, striving to squeeze every ounce of meaning and persuasion out of it. With each repetition, Popolitipov draws closer to her—and draws her closer to him. The word acts as a mantra, embedding itself into the ear of the listener:

Love   Love   Love   Love   Love

The interpretive road is wide open for the actor. For instance, the word "love" can escalate rhythmically in its impact, almost like a crescendo, gaining incremental emphasis, or the word can continually change its shape, searching for ever more vivid meanings:

love   **love**   Love   Love   *Love*

It's as if the speaker is discovering richer and deeper layers of meaning with each repetition. Try this little speech and see if you can make each repetition count, delivering a distinct or incremental payoff to the pattern of epizeuxis. Remember, Popolitipov is attempting to win over a very reluctant, jaded, and utterly disinterested young woman. He understands the obstacles before him; he is not interested in casual chitchat (nor are many of Kushner's characters), and so he cranks up his commitment to word power. He bares his soul, pours forth his feelings, yes, but he ultimately calls upon language to describe the world and reinforce his deepest desires.

Down and out, adrift in a meaningless existence encased by his coarse low-end blue-collar neighborhood, Joey lashes out against his girlfriend's paralysis, her timidity, in Jim Cartwright's play *Road*.

> You're just like all the rest of them. Frightened to sniff the wind for fear it'll blow your brain upside down....Wasting your whole lives. Work, work, work, work, work. Small wages, small wages, small wages. Gettin' by with a smile. Gettin' by without a smile. Work, work, work, work. Small wages. Then death with the Big "D."
>
> (Act 1)

Chapter Five

The cascade of repetitive words embodies the dull routine of a mediocre, unconscious life. The obsessive mantra of "work, work, work, work, work" followed by "small wages, small wages, small wages" provides a fast-forward movie of an empty life, devoid of meaning. Language drives character. The actor can exploit this rhetorical figure in performance, bravely playing the repetition, rather than avoiding it or apologizing for its "excess." Its *excess* is the point. It fuels Joey's compulsion and message. Play with escalating rhythm and increasing urgency. Bite the words, spit them out with the venom they demand. Remember, the character *craves* the repetition, the lifeblood of his argument.

Outrageous Mantras

In Tim Kochendurfer's play *The Search for Cindy*, the ever-changeable Cindy tells her shocked boyfriend, Tim, that she is breaking up with him, reminding him of her propensity for boredom. "So, that's it. It's over?" asks a bewildered Tim. Cindy loads her repeating rifle and fires.

> No, no, no. We can still be really, really, really, really, really, really, really, really good friends.

What an escalation! Here, the repetitive barrage gathers progressive strength, claiming greater and greater outrageous emphasis—and ignites some absurdist humor at its conclusion. It's as if each repetition incrementally increases the compensation for the severed relationship! So the actor should not simply race through the repetition but should use the momentum and increasing emphasis of epizeuxis to convince the down-in-the-dumps boyfriend of her boundless commitment to superhuman friendship, however insincere or fabricated such a bloated declaration may be.

For the ultimate wild ride of epizeuxis, we must look to Tristan Tzara in Tom Stoppard's ideological slugfest, *Travesties*. Tristan Tzara, founder of the anti-art movement, **Dada**, seeks to debunk all of Henry Carr's serious sentiments about war, cause and effect, and art. The true artist, Tzara insists, should jeer and scoff at pious scientific explanations and traditional values, like sentimental art. Tzara champions random chance, nihilism, the bringing down of old creaky structures and thinking. The duty of the artist, counters Henry Carr, is to "beautify existence." And then Tristan Tzara unloads an off-the-scale bombardment, pounding the stage with an unforgettably crazed mantra.

> Dada dada dada dada dada dada dada dada
> dada dada dada dada dada dada dada dada
> dada dada dada dada dada dada dada dada
> dada dada dada dada dada dada dada dada
> dada dada.
> (Act 2)

Dada, the wickedly nonsensical word that celebrates the wickedly nonsensical world view of Tzara, is given room to rage. What is the actor to do with this shameless verbal display? *Play with it.* Stretch it like children's clay, slow it down, speed it up, pound it like a drum, boom it like a tuba, croon it like a vaudeville tune. Dada celebrates babble, sound and rhythm; it shuns traditional meaning, preferring the bravery of pure expression. As such, this passage encourages the performer to soar with the high-flying ones, to check inhibition at the back stage door. And yet it is not total nonsense. Dada is responding to the serious world here, rattling off a defiant and delightful cuckoo spell to the well-worn habits and thoughts of a society too comfortable with itself.

Grab a little playfulness—and give Tzara a whirl.

Mixing It Up

We have thus far examined repetitive strategies individually. However, these strategies may work in tandem in a given text. Our three key figures—Epimone, Palilogia, Epizeuxis—can team up to provide a powerful punch, continually jabbing and accenting key ideas. In Zell Miller III's spoken word performance piece, *The Evidence of Silence Broken*, the zealous black Poet recalls an encounter on a city bus.

> Once on the back of a bus. a man, average man, suit-wearing man, suit-wearing man, wanted to sit down, sit down next to me.

Chapter Five

> suit-wearing man in white skin and wet hair, and long day, looking for a sit down, suit-wearing man said: "May I sit down." black man, me. black man in revolutionary mode. I. revolutionary mode. me. saw white man as reflection of all white men. in search of change, me: "By any means necessary," misquote. me. acted no better than them who I wanted to change / kill / teach. see learned oppression from an oppressor. but this man. this average man, suit-wearing man. only wanted to sit down.

Look at the variety of repetitive spells and grooves. This Poet, in the heat of racial tension, ignites every thought with repetition, primarily using the delayed spell of epimone and the reinforcement of palilogia. Although the whole speech seems wrapped in compulsive epizeuxis. His repetitive hammer brings our attention to details we might have missed or taken for granted. "Suit-wearing man"—in its constant reminder—becomes a totem for the white establishment he distrusts and despises. This average, suit-wearing man simply wants to "sit down," but for the Poet, this act conjures images from Montgomery bus boycotts and is therefore a revolutionary one, and in his "revolutionary mode" he views this act as a direct challenge. And despite his considerable self-awareness, later in the speech, the Poet cannot help but shout a command.

> You stand your ass up, my people had to stand for four hundred years, so you stand your punk ass up.

More reinforcement. The second utterance strengthens the first. As this "average man, suit-wearing man" turns away and stands, the Poet initially feels a sense of victory. And in a fascinating turnaround, the Poet then describes the realization—in later years—of his own misunderstanding of that average man, that suit-wearing man "looking for a sit down." Remarkably, the phrase "suit-wearing man" travels many miles in this speech, from a kind of anonymous symbol of oppression to an unwitting or unsuspecting figure:

SUIT-WEARING MAN! → suit-wearing man

Practice this speech aloud and let it work on you. Try to avoid interpretive judgments prior to speaking the text aloud. Its repetitive structure will take you to unexpected places if you are open to its influence. Language-driven actor training allows space for the words themselves to shape character.

Palilogia, the *Reinforcer*, and Epizeuxis, the *Mantra*, are a powerful team. One provides a quick punch, the other an extended pummeling. Epimone works its magic through delay. All three derive power from the vehemence unleashed by the act of verbal repetition. They also celebrate the exploration of a word's meaning by its very repetition. They are not content with a one-time utterance of a phrase or word. All are too passionate for such economy. These verbal strategies seek a *zealous actor*, one who demands the repeated attack, works with degrees of emphasis, and verbally insists that the phrase is worth repeating.

REPETITION OF IDEAS

COMMORATIO
The Sharpener

"I know I have been wicked, odious, bad," cries the slyly penitent Julia in Bernard Shaw's *The Philanderer*. Ideas often clamor for recapitulation, for an extra sharpening of the blade. How often do we refine an idea by rephrasing it, providing two or three additional versions? It's as if the supplemental versions provide a greater sting to the root idea. In the same way that we are often not satisfied with saying a word only once, feeling a strong urge to repeat it, we are equally dissatisfied with a one-time expression of an idea, wanting further elaboration. Not only can words repeat, but so can ideas. With **Commoratio** (ko mo RAH tee o), *the speaker stresses a main point by repeating it in different words, sharpening it several times for razor-like emphasis*.

For the actor, commoratio is a tool of verbal **drive** and **slicing emphasis**. It both shapes a sentence and launches it forward with renewed energy.

In Charles Mee's play *bobrauschenbergamerica*, a kaleidoscope of American images, characters, and cultural fragments as imagined through the lens of the artist Robert Rauschenberg, a woman named Susan spies a disheveled derelict in the distance. At first glance, she seems repulsed by him.

Chapter Five

>get this fellow away from me
>lock him up, put him away
>send him to an island
>you know, the island of the damned,
>the island of the rejects
>whatever
>just get him out of here.
> (Scene 6)

Bursts of commoratio power this dialogue. The imperative, "get this fellow away from me," is repeated three times, in different ways. We can diagram it:

>*Main point:* **Get this fellow away from me**
>→lock him up
>**→put him away**
>**→send him to an island**

Three distinct but related versions back up the main point. Each one pushes the sentence forward and reinvigorates it. The actor can attack each repeating idea by giving each phrase a separate vocal accent or emphasis, not letting the sentence sink into the quicksand of inner pauses, reflections, and spur-of-the-moment "searching" for an idea. These contemporary habits blunt the power of repetition. Each restatement increases the urgency of Susan's command and heightens her revulsion—and that is why she is not content with a one-time utterance of her main point. Susan needs the bolstering impact of commoratio to fully express her desire to rid herself of the derelict's company.

She continues with another dose of commoratio in the next few lines. "Send him to an island," she demands:

>**→the island of the *damned***
>**→the island of *rejects***

"Misfits" is her theme and she riffs on it, slicing her way to further refinement. She concludes with her original point: "Just get him out of here." The strategy of commoratio is to continually pass the blade of an idea against the whetstone

MANTRAS, SPELLS, AND GROOVES: Repetition

of restatement. The effect is to arrest the listener with an ever-sharpening series of verbal thrusts, keeping him alert, on his toes, fully engaged.

The characters of *bobrauschenbergamerica* frequently call upon this verbal strategy to chisel their thoughts and heighten the urgency of their communication. The frustrated Wilson speaks to Susan, with whom he is having an illicit affair.

> I can't help myself loving you
> and then you go back to your husband again
> so it turns out
> the only way I can keep you is by making you feel anxious
> keeping you on edge
> making you feel I'm about to drop you
> (Scene 18)

Frustrated by the topsy-turvy, on-again, off-again relationship with a woman who slips away when she senses his devotion, Wilson realizes Susan becomes closer when he creates insecurity. He reveals his main point and strategy:

making you feel anxious

This idea is sharpened and propelled by two restatements:

➔**keeping you on edge**
➔**making you feel I'm about to drop you**

The actor must take advantage of the additional firepower bolstering the key idea. Again, each restatement ratchets up the urgency, the persuasive potential of the argument. Each one "pierces" the listener with a renewed vigor. Commoratio does not yield time for introspective moodiness. If the actor has three arrows in his quiver, each arrow should be distinct yet flying toward the same target—with increasing drive and zest.

One of the defining features of Oscar Wilde's dialogue is the way in which his characters continually refine a thought, never content to merely paint a single brushstroke but to reinforce it with complementary hues. In *An Ideal Husband*, Gertrude Chiltern learns the origins of her esteemed husband's

Chapter Five

wealth and political career—fraud and corruption. As a young man, Sir Robert Chiltern sold a cabinet secret to a scheming baron, profiting handsomely from the insider information it contained. Gertrude is crushed by the revelation, as her idealized image of Robert dissolves: "Oh what a mask you have been wearing all these years!" Her humiliation is painful, as she realizes her "worship" of him was an illusion. Sir Robert, in a wrenching monologue, attempts to mount a defense.

> You made your false idol of me, and I had not the courage to come down, show you my wounds, tell you my weaknesses.
> (Act 2)

After repeating the idea of weakness or injury, Sir Robert blames his wife for interfering with his blackmailer, the charmingly treacherous Mrs. Cheveley, whose possession of an incriminating letter provides proof of Sir Robert's crime. This "sin of my youth," he notes, could have been buried once and for all.

> I could have killed it forever, sent it back into its tomb, destroyed its record, burned the one witness against me. You prevented me.

Look at how the main idea, **"I could have killed it forever,"** is accented by three barbed accomplices:

→ **sent it back into its tomb**
→ **destroyed its record**
→ **burned the one witness against me**

Sir Robert follows this point with his greatest display of restatement.

> And now what is there before me but public disgrace, ruin, terrible shame, the mockery of the world, a lonely, dishonoured life, a lonely, dishonoured death, it may be, some day?

Disgrace and dishonor sliced into various shapes. His entire monologue is activated and spurred by the rhetorical strategy of commoratio. Sir Robert's seething mind is grappling with the life-changing ramifications of a dark

MANTRAS, SPELLS, AND GROOVES: Repetition

past now brought to light—and his continual craving for repetition reflects a temperament flushing out all possible nuances of his fate. In this context, his rising desperation is well matched by his reliance on compulsive restatement.

EXERGASIA
Big Workout

When an idea is extended over a lengthy passage, repeated in a variety of ways, it is propelled by *exergasia*, a close ally of commoratio. **Exergasia** (ex er GAY see a), the Greek word for "working out," occurs when the speaker seeks *a wide variety of images and viewpoints to illumine a single idea or thought*. The idea is "worked out" through repetition. The emphasis here is on the speaker's ability to gather a diverse range of perspectives—and put them in the service of one idea. Exergasia, really, is a more elaborate and complex version of commoratio.

One of the most riveting examples of exergasia occurs in the opening soliloquy of Shakespeare's *Richard III*. Richard describes his lusty brother, King Edward, who now enjoys the throne, and who now dallies with suppliant young courtesans in his bed chamber, wallowing in erotic luxury. Then Richard turns the camera on himself, striking a strong contrast with his older brother.

> But I, that am not shap'd for sportive tricks,
> Nor made to court an amorous looking-glass;
> I, that am rudely stamp'd, and want love's majesty
> To strut before a wanton ambling nymph;
> I, that am curtail'd of this fair proportion,
> Cheated of feature by dissembling nature,
> Deform'd, unfinish'd, sent before my time
> Into this breathing world, scarce half made up,
> —And that so lamely and unfashionable
> That dogs bark at me as I halt by them—
> Why I in this weak piping time of peace,

Chapter Five

> Have no delight to pass away the time,
> Unless to spy my shadow in the sun
> And descant on my own deformity.
>
> (1.1)

A repetitive masterpiece, these fourteen lines comprise one sentence (!) and one essential idea—physical **deformity**. But look at the multitude of ways Richard grabs hold of this idea. Deformity is viewed from a variety of angles, particularly images suggesting an imbalance or disharmony with Nature, a vital Elizabethan concept. Richard continually riffs on his physical appearance in an arresting sequence:

- → I, that am not shap'd for *sportive tricks*   [*sexual games*]
- → Nor made to court an amorous looking-glass;
- → rudely stamp'd
- → want [*lack*] love's majesty to strut before a wanton ambling nymph
- → curtail'd of this fair *proportion*   [*harmony*]
- → cheated of feature by dissembling nature
- → deform'd
- → unfinish'd
- → sent before my time/ Into this breathing world, scarce half made up   [*premature birth*]
- → spy my shadow in the sun/ And descant on my own deformity.

What a **workout!** Ten distinct viewpoints illumine Richard's physical state, his supposed ugliness. Richard first opines about his body, finding it unfit for "sportive tricks," describing it as "rudely stamp'd" and ill-suited for "love's majesty." He then embarks on a chain of images suggesting that Nature has cheated him of a "fair proportion," ordained his premature birth—"sent before my time/ Into this breathing world, scarce half made up." In a graphic aside, Richard notes that even dogs bark at him as he limps by. He ends with an image of his deformed silhouette in shadow.

How can the actor use this "workout" to enhance his performance? First, it is absolutely critical to note that these fourteen lines comprise one essential idea—deformity—and that these fourteen lines comprise one sentence.

MANTRAS, SPELLS, AND GROOVES: Repetition

These two observations work in tandem. Exergasia signals a kind of obsession, a feverish desire to continually reexamine an idea, from different angles. So the speech must drive, propel, slice, emphasize each new angle and image of Deformity. Fully absorbed by his subject, Richard refuses to slacken the repetitive tension; instead, he keeps scratching for new images. Remember, he needs each image to build his case, to have us believe that his motives are shaped by his exterior state. (Whether we accept this reasoning is another matter.) Indeed, he must eagerly track down all ten descriptions: "Look at this image—now look at this graphic image—here's another view of my handicap—wake up!—here's yet another glance at my cursed lot."

The speech uses the power of repetition to increase its momentum, build an inexorable logic, and make emphatic distinctions. For Richard, each image and each verse line is indispensable, and each serves one master—Physical Appearance. The actor must share this zealotry and recognition. He cannot play ten separate intentions and he cannot lose sight of the goalpost. Repetition shapes this soliloquy, gives it palpable form. In this speech, *exergasia is character*, and the actor can exploit the repetitive verbal craft to drive and highlight the essence of Richard's argument.

Hunger for repetition is what ultimately shapes commoratio—and its ally exergasia—and the actor's response to this figure. Are you hungry enough to use it? Or do you throw it away as an unnecessary piece of fluff? Do you see it as an ally for theatrical power and expression, for persuasion? If so, exergasia and commoratio are key tools for sharpening the blade of a gathering thought, one restatement at a time.

REPETITION OF STRUCTURE, SOUND

Finally, we will examine two figures that represent the repetition of structure and sound, respectively. These are fundamentally **Figures of Rhythm**. Both, in different ways, propel an intoxicating sense of rhythm and bounce and are wonderful tools for the actor to employ in the art of persuasive speaking.

Chapter Five

ISOCOLON
The Benny Goodman Figure

With his cards spread out on the table, playing before an imaginary crowd, Lincoln prepares to give his younger brother a lesson in the street hustle called three-card monte, in Suzan-Lori Parks' *Topdog/Underdog*. Lincoln knows this con game depends on a hypnotic sense of rhythm, sleight of hand, and a cool persona. Above all, Lincoln knows the voice plays a crucial role in the persuasion of the cards.

> There's 2 parts to throwing thuh cards. Both parts are fairly complicated. Thuh moves and thuh grooves, thuh talk and thuh walk, thuh patter and thuh pitter pat, thuh flap and thuh rap: what yr doing with yr mouth and what yr doing with yr hands.
>
> (Scene 5)

He begins his lesson with a rhythmic groove, shuffling the cards in sync with his voice. His neatly symmetrical phrases tap out an overt rhythmic beat:

> **Thuh moves and the grooves**
> **thuh talk and the thuh walk**
> **thuh patter and the pitter pat**
> **thuh flap and thuh rap**
>
> **what yr doing with yr hands**
> **what yr doing with yr mouth**

Notice that the first sequence features phrases that share the same repeated grammatical structure, Noun and Noun, and are identical in length. The second sequence features two phrases that contain the same structure and the same length.

As rhythmic creatures, human beings love the Groove, the Beat—which are created and sustained by repetition. Music seduces our ear—and body—with its array of repeating motifs, cadences, and phrases, which sweep us into a delightful groove. Language, as verbally hip playwrights know, can do the same thing. The listener may accept an idea more readily if it comes packaged

MANTRAS, SPELLS, AND GROOVES: Repetition

in a rhythmic, foot-tapping way. One of the key figures celebrating this notion is **Isocolon** (eye so COE lun), meaning "of equal members." Isocolon generates a *tremendous "rhythmic swing" by stringing together a series of clauses which repeat the same grammatical structure and length.* These "*word chunks*" build an infectious groove, one that the actor can play.

In the preceding example, Lincoln uses rhyme to help bolster the word chunks, but isocolon often plays solo, drawing on rhythm alone to work its magic. In John Marston's early 17th-century play *The Malcontent*, a hilarious exposé of Machiavellian intrigue in the Court of Genoa, the court lackey Mendoza revels in his status as minion to the duchess. His access to power makes him gloat over "petitionary vassals licking the pavement with their slavish knees." But he especially treasures his newfound access to the duchess. Furthermore, he now has access to all of the women at court. "O Paradise!" screams Mendoza. Utterly inspired, he dashes off a ravishing description of "sweet women, most sweet ladies, nay, angels!"

> In body how delicate, in soul how witty, in discourse how pregnant, in life how wary, in favours how judicious, in day how sociable, and in night how—O pleasure unutterable!
>
> (1.5)

This language jumps off the page! Listen to how Mendoza uses the rhythmic zest of isocolon to build his escalating excitement. He "swings" the rhythm to a climax. The language craves an actor who can read its cues and take it to the top:

> **In body how delicate**
> **in soul how witty**
> **in discourse how pregnant**
> **in life how wary**
> **in favours how judicious**
> **in day how sociable**
> **and in night how—O pleasure unutterable!**

The structure, Noun and Adjective, is repeated throughout. The length of each phrase is roughly the same. Note that the length of the phrases need not

Chapter Five

be identical but simply close in duration, to preserve the cadence. Two key precepts govern the actor's use of this buoyant figure:

✔ **Phrase it**
✔ **Swing it**

Phrasing, or knowing "what goes with what," is mandatory. "In body how delicate" is one phrase. "In soul how witty" is another distinct phrase. Each phrase must be sliced neatly away from the preceding phrase.

> **When one phrase blurs into the next, the rhythm is lost and the ear can no longer pick up the infectious cadence.**

It should now be evident why the contemporary habit of random pausing in the *middle of a phrase* will not serve the demands of isocolon:

> **In body how…delicate**
> **in soul…how……witty**
> **in…life…how wary**
> **in favours…how…judicious**

The film-oriented, naturalistic habit of "searching" for the right word, as if the word were spontaneously conjured, wipes out the rhythmic appeal of this figure. This contemporary habit proves fatal here. Can you see how Mendoza's language knows where it is going and does not need soul searching? The phrases are already "loaded" into the mouth of the speaker—and he lets them fly.

With phrasing comes the ability to swing. Look at how Mendoza strings together an intoxicating sequence. Each phrase is distinct, yet it anticipates the next phrase, handing off energy and verve to its successor. Taken as a whole, the sequence soars rhythmically, proceeds on a delightfully arching tangent to the climactic top. In the American Big Band jazz era, this sensation was called "swing," a feeling that the tempo was subtly picking up speed, moving with an inexorable energy that pulled the listener onto the pulsing dance floor. Like the famous jazz clarinetist Benny Goodman, the King of Swing, Mendoza plays a thrilling, infectious riff:

MANTRAS, SPELLS, AND GROOVES: Repetition

> O pleasure unutterable!
> and in night how—
> in day how sociable
> in favours how judicious
> in life how wary
> in discourse how pregnant
> in soul how witty
> In body how delicate

Give this sequence a go. You will notice that you will occasionally need a quick catch-breath *in the gap between* two phrases. At other times you will be able to get through two or three phrases on one breath. In either case, follow the phrasing—and it will help you achieve a gathering momentum. Does each phrase propel you to the next? Are you starting to discover a rhythm to this sequence? Swing is a fantastic groove that the audience wants to ride. Shake yourself out, put on your blue suede shoes, and spin these phrases across the ballroom floor. Keep in mind the subject of Mendoza's verbal romp, his excited state, and you will be reminded of the sustained energy necessary to zing this sequence. At the same time, the actor is asked to provide some vocal variety to the parade of nouns and adjectives, so that "body" and "delicate," for instance, are distinct from "soul" and "witty."

Swing Dance

Flash forward four hundred years to the 21st century, into the quirky romantic landscape of Melanie Marnich's *Quake*, where Lucy is on a quest to find Mr. Right. She thinks she finds him at an elevation of 30,000 feet, sitting next to her on a Delta flight to Denver. After a smattering of introductory chitchat, they begin to lock eyes, turning up the heat between them. Lucy begins to touch him, as they describe one another's attractive features. In the stage directions, the playwright notes that the "rhythm builds." Isoco, on, specifically, builds it.

> ROGER: And I say yes—
> LUCY: To your lips.

Chapter Five

    ROGER: To your eyes.
    LUCY: To your breath.
    ROGER: To your cheeks.
    LUCY: To your nipples.
    ROGER: Dimples.
    LUCY: Tendons, ankles, toes.
    (*Hotter rhythm*)
    ROGER: And I say touch.
    LUCY: And I say kiss.
    ROGER: And I say teeth.
    LUCY: And I say tongue.
    ROGER: And I say start.
    LUCY: And I say go.
    ROGER: And I say now.
    LUCY: And I say slow.
    ROGER: And I say soft.
    LUCY: And I say make—
    ROGER: Me—
    LUCY: Stay.

                                              (Scene 9)

This is a swinging *pas de deux*! Both actors have to stay "in tempo" and have to spur each other on, lindy hopping with increasing speed and energy. It is truly a dance, where both performers must "feel" each other verbally as well as emotionally. It's an exciting sequence to play. Either actor can break the dance by not listening and not responding to the partner's verbal cues. Now, the isocolon run, in this particular sequence, is aided by word repetition as well, but the primary rhythmic responsibility lies with structural repetition.

    Isocolon comes in all shapes and sizes. Sometimes the rhythmic elements are short and pithy, likes Caesar's famously infectious remark following his quick victory over Pharnaces, at the Battle of Zela: Veni, Vidi, Vici (I came, saw, conquered). Verb-Verb-Verb, at two syllables apiece. Backed by alliteration. At other times, the structure is a bit longer, as when a heavy metal rocker says, "I jammed all night, slept all morning, partied 'til dawn." Whatever the size or shape, isocolon asks the performer to use its inherent rhythmic symmetry. Not to bury it with introspective moodiness. Isocolon celebrates rhythm as a necessary adjunct of meaning. People are instinctively attracted to a message wrapped in a beat. They listen with their bodies as well as with their minds. The Big Band swing era musician Benny Goodman knew that secret. Today's actor can reclaim this secret for the American theater.

HOMOIOTELUETON
The Hip-Hop Figure

Backed by a DJ's sampled beats, a disciplined visual artist, Stephen, describes his wariness as an attractive young dancer-choreographer, Sisha, moves into a studio across the hall from his own cloistered workspace, in Kim Euell's *The Dance*.

> I'm sensing potential distraction/ a major infraction/ to creative satisfaction/ But I had me some traction/ my strategy?/ simple/ cut it off at the source/ always checking the halls before venturing forth/ in case someone was on patrol/ to snatch an unwary heart and soul/
>
> (1.4, "Obsession")

These hip-hoppin' phrases have an unmistakable groove, accompanied by a humorous undertow. And the lyrics have that ring of repetition. The words celebrate repetition of *sound*. Specifically, they celebrate the *endings* of words, which is where the repetition is found:

- distrac-*tion*
- infrac-*tion*
- satisfac-*tion*
- trac-*tion*

Two thousand five hundred years ago, the ancient peoples of the Mediterranean also celebrated this particular kind of sound repetition—and named it *homoioteleuton*. Take a deep breath; this word looks much scarier than it actually is. **Ho mo ee te LOOT on**. *It means "same endings" and it*

Chapter Five

derives its power from the seductive chemistry created when word endings continually collide in similar sounds.

The ancient Greeks knew that Homoioteleuton was a rhythmic figure and, as such, had a special appeal in the pantheon of persuasion. There is something engaging about a sequence of phrases that feature similar sounding endings. The mind and ear get caught up in a kind of groove, falling into the beat of the message, bopping their assent. Hip-Hop artists love this figure; it is one of the key figures in their voracious verbal arsenal. They lean into these word endings with an extra **stress** or **punch** so that the sound can be "picked up" in succeeding words.

This sound play is often featured in plays with overt rhetorical display. In William Congreve's Restoration comedy *The Way of the World*, two refined ladies, fans-a-fluttering, meet in the park to discuss the latest romantic vexations.

> MRS. MARWOOD: You hate mankind?
> MRS. FAINALL: Heartily, inveterately.
> MRS. MARWOOD: Your husband?
> MRS. FAINALL: Most transcendently; aye, though I say it, meritoriously.
>
> (2.1)

Notice how Mrs. Fainall subtly stresses the "ly" endings to push the dialogue forward: *heartily, inveterately, transcendently, meritoriously*. Homoioteleuton instigates verbal energy, generates a sweeping rhythmic momentum by accenting the repetition of sounds. The actor must recognize this vitality of sound in rhetorically crafted dialogue. Much of the charm—and wit—of Mrs. Fainall's lines resides in her use of sound and rhythm. How many repeated word endings can she string together? Homoioteleuton, at heart, always has a bit of swagger to it, an attitude of bravura. "Check out this catchy sequence!" the speaker says to her audience.

The Oscar for the most dazzling display of sound endings goes to Miss Cecily in Tom Stoppard's *Travesties*. Cecily, a devoted Leninist librarian, extols the virtues of Marxist doctrine, climbing onto her desk in a rapturous tribute.

MANTRAS, SPELLS, AND GROOVES: Repetition

The only way is the way of Marx and of Lenin, the enemy of all revisionism!—of opportunist liberal economism!—of social-chauvinist bourgeois individualism!—quasi-Dadaist paternalism!—pseudo-Wildean aphorism!—sub-Joycean catechism and dogmatism!—cubism!—expressionism!—rheumatism!

(Act 2)

This unrelenting stampede of "isms" would make the most indulgent rapper green with envy. Homoioteleuton powers this speech, generating its absurd zeal, fueling its world-shattering logic. It is a workout! This gathering wave keeps coming, keeps insisting on its ludicrously righteous momentum. For the performer, there are several key challenges. Cecily must not peak too soon, but must steadily ratchet up the roll call of debunked political philosophies—the various "isms"—as she slices her way through history. Above all, the actor must not apologize for verbal excess. She cannot blur or hurry through the roll call, in an "excuse me" bow to naturalism and its narrow straits. On the contrary, the word endings must be openly exploited, lit up with vocal neon, flashed before the eyes and ears of the spectators.

Homoioteleuton, the Hip-Hop figure, is a catchy, rhythmic device, one that has grooved its way across the millennia, from Sophocles to Jay-Z. This figure understands that the human ear is "hooked" by repetition of sound. It reminds us that, for all our towering intellect, we are still creatures of the beat, of the chemistry of sound, of play. When packing her suitcase for a role, the actor is asked to leave a little space for this rhythmic awareness.

TAKING STOCK

Repetition is a strategic response to the challenge of human persuasion. Whether the actor casts a spell, by voicing a recurring phrase, or whether she chants an obsessively repeating mantra—or simply rephrases an idea, the actor is seeking the seductive charisma of reinforcement, restatement, vehemence. Repetition is a bold wake-up signal, a flash of electric communication that asks the listener to take a second look, and maybe a third or fourth look. It insists the communication *needs* that second look. The actor must prove

Chapter Five

this insistence as well, using the voice—and a zealous attitude—to take advantage of repetition. Don't let that dramatic opportunity pass by. Justify that refrain, sharpen that reoccurring idea, make us hear the difference between the first and second utterance.

Swing those repeating rhythms and sounds, and you will find the groove that invites the listener's body, as well as mind, to move with the spirit of your communication.

Repetition is a fervent ally, one that the actor can embrace and hold on to as the carousel goes around…and around…and around.

Chapter Six

TRUSTING THE LANGUAGE

A thrilling charge. That's what potent orchestrated language injects into human communication and storytelling. It jolts us out of the ordinary and into an atmosphere brimming with dramatic wonder. We have seen how the forgotten art of rhetoric offers actors exciting opportunities to "light up" the arena, to spark the imagination of the listener and thus create the context for persuasion. The previous chapters show how verbal figures heighten, embolden, and inspire a piece of communication. Whether stretching language, powering words, evoking a verbal cinema, making connections, or repeating a spell, the actor is using the fireworks of rhetoric to woo the consent of the audience. The words blaze high into the sky and explode with myriad colors and shapes, to our delight and astonishment.

That's really the point. In ages past, speakers knew that words were astonishing—and *magical*. That is, they knew that the ultimate effect of a pleasing verbal sequence may not subscribe to rational explanation or analysis. How can we really explain the mysterious appeal or power of metaphor, for example? When Richard III substitutes "winter of our discontent" for war and "glorious summer" for peace, we are pleased, enchanted, lifted up. Exactly why that is, well, it eludes scientific reasoning. The language strikes a magical chord in us. We are drawn to it. Listen to a dramatically surging piece of music, one that starts simply and builds incrementally into a raging storm. A crescendo. Our bodies are roused and instilled with a palpable passion. We lean forward and forget our tired state and our sundry personal anxieties. We are lifted up. That's magical. Verbal amplifying runs, as we have seen, provide the same crescendo. The speaker's propulsive words charge up the mountain and, when the sentence crests the top, we instinctually applaud. We give our consent.

We observed how patterns of repetition, like King's "I have a dream" refrain, cast a spell upon the listener, tapping into an ancient and mysterious precinct of our human imagination. These patterns are captivating. All of

Chapter Six

the rhetorical figures featured in this book are capable of such enchantment. They do not live in the realm of drab ordinariness but in the brilliant hues of extraordinary communication. Rhetorical figures have survived through the ages precisely because they have this incandescent, magical power to elicit our agreement.

From a large and exhaustive list of rhetorical devices, this book has selected a relatively small number, the ones that actors are likely to find most useful on stage, in performance. They are meant to be spoken aloud. They come alive in the mouths and voices of actors, in the speaking. They are not necessarily the same figures one would find in a literature class, where students dissect the symbolic strategy of the author, without ever listening, in many cases, to the voice leave the body. The selected figures can be put to practical use immediately, in the sound and fury of a courageous stage performance. They are not theoretical devices; they are practical tools that enliven human speaking and energize audience listening. These figures take on persuasive power as they soar across the footlights into the ears and minds of the listeners.

For the sake of clarity and introductory simplicity, we have focused on rhetorical figures one device at a time. However, actors may often discover several figures working in tandem in a speech or scene. In Tony Kushner's *Slavs!*, Katherina Gleb contrasts her partner, Dr. Bonfila Bonch-Bruevich, with a corrupt Soviet government official, who has been attempting to seduce her. She gives him a stinging rebuke.

> And she is a physician, she cures people, not an ineffectual aged paperpushing-timeserver-apparatchik-with-a-dacha like you who only bleeds the people dry.
>
> (2.1)

This passage combines antithesis with accumulatio. For antithetical stretch, Katherina opposes the government official (Popolitipov) to Dr. Bonfila:

Dr. Bonfila	Popolitipov
physician	ineffectual aged
cures people	paperpushing timeserver
	apparatchik
	bleeds people dry

The description of Popolitipov, the second half of the antithesis, is an accumulating run, one that gathers rhythmic force and verbal drive as it reaches the summit—"bleeds the people dry." So, an accumulatio wrapped inside an antithesis! As you can see, rhetorical figures can arrive in many combinations and guises.

Verbal Awareness and Preparation

This book has suggested that crafted verbal power represents a lost and potent knowledge that we can recover today and employ in the contemporary theater. To take full advantage of this lost art, we can start with a new appreciation for "visible" language in the theater, whether old or new, a language that openly calls attention to its attitude, its calculated parade of glossy words. It does not merely see itself as a transparent window onto the world. Quite the contrary, crafted language, be it by Stoppard, Shaw, Shakespeare, or Parks, creates a significant part of the dramatic experience of the play. The words do not merely reflect the world; they shape the world. One tosses them aside at one's peril. In their feverish pursuit of subtext and characterization, today's actors often neglect the language in verbally adventurous plays, fail to see that the words themselves are forming the experience of the play.

So how can today's actor begin to increase awareness of the *verbal surface*? A good starting point asks performers to do what so many schoolkids did for centuries. Write original examples. That's right, jot down your own original version of, say, antithesis, accumulatio, epimone. By composing your own antithesis, for example, you will begin to build verbal muscle and memory. As the composer of your own metaphorical "run" or passage of "verbal cinema," you will begin to gain insights into the very structure of verbal craft, sharpening your awareness and understanding of how these figures work in performance. Speak your composition aloud, be bold, revel in your choices. You will begin to see how verbal style reflects personality—a key ingredient in understanding character.

Next, pick a speech by Shaw or Shakespeare, for instance, and start speaking. Take it one line at a time. Avoid any preordained choices about character or action. In fact, for the sake of experimentation, consciously decline to play a "character." Rely simply on your own voice and ability to speak the lines.

Chapter Six

Let the lines work on you. The language may surprise you, nudge or drag you in a direction you may not have anticipated. Let the images, the rhetorical structures, the sounds and rhythms guide you. (You will have plenty of opportunities, later, to pour in your character work.) For starters, you are simply tasting the words, getting a feel for the essential "story" of the piece. What is s/he saying? How is the language informing and revealing the story? Speak the speech numerous times. Give your trust to the text, lean on it, be receptive to its twists and turns. Is the persuasion of the story becoming sharper and clearer?

As you heighten your awareness of rhetorical devices and verbal craft, you will simultaneously increase your commitment to passionate communication, to the hunger of expression. Verbal craft is persuasive but it does not exist in a vacuum: It is best accompanied by a ravenous desire to instill in the listener each detail of the story. The speaker has a zealous commitment to paint each image, realize every nuance. Simply put, the speaker must have a powerful passion to communicate.

Actors can strengthen this intention and make it more vivid. Find an episode from your own life experience that is absolutely riveting or exhilarating. It may have involved joy or danger or breathtaking surprise—but you experienced the event in a moment-to-moment, I'm-alive-right-now kind of way. Write up this episode in short monologue form and perform it for friends. Remember, you want them to experience the "aliveness" you experienced. You don't want them to miss any of it. You want them to hang on to every sentence and detail. In performing this piece, you may find unexpected corridors of expression, vocal stretch, as you discover a new appreciation for what it really takes to communicate. You will also be creating the context in which rhetorical figures can thrive.

Striking a Balance: Language and Behavior

Throughout the chapters of this book, we have suggested that an increased verbal awareness can help guide actors to richer characterization and expression.

At the same time, it is important to acknowledge that this verbal approach to performance is seemingly at odds with some of contemporary theater's most hallowed precepts about character and interpretation. Actors are often urged to look beneath the text, finding behavioral clues in the so-called subtext. They are prompted to explore the character's intentions, the emotional undercurrents, hidden feelings, and desires—*as if they existed independently of the words themselves*. (Remember, some acting methodologies have stated, "It's not about the words.") In this strategy, behavioral exhibition or emotion tends to wallop the words in performance. That is, the words are treated as a whipping post for the character's inner life and display of feelings.

Might we find a better balance between words and behavior?

Let's look at a concrete example. Bernard Shaw's *Saint Joan* is an excellent case in point. The play is brimming with powerful language and powerful emotion. Shaw, as usual, has composed a brilliantly crafted text, and yet the issues in the play conjure deep wells of feeling and even ecstasy. Toward the end of the play, Joan is put on trial for heresy and is pronounced guilty. This young uneducated country girl, who roused her people to rise up against an occupier, has dared to suggest that her inspiration and courage come directly from God and his angels, without the intercession of the formal Church and its hierarchy. God speaks directly to her.

Such dangerous heresy or "opinion," the ecclesiastical court finds, must be condemned and cast out. Otherwise, a precedent of romantic anarchy would be established, whereby any delirious and self-possessed zealot could claim similar divine inspiration, outside the sanctions of the Church. Joan is courageous, charismatic, and iron-willed, yet she is also politically naïve, incapable of grasping how her individualistic stance puts her on a collision course with the ominous structures of authority during the Inquisition. She pays the ultimate price for her *opinion*. She is sentenced to burn at the stake.

Joan finally agrees to sign a confession, naïvely believing that her signature will set her free. When told that it merely saves her from the fire, that she will now live the rest of her life in prison, subsisting on bread and water, Joan is outraged. She rips her signed confession, tells the court to prepare her fire, and speaks:

> You promised me my life; but you lied. You think that life is nothing but not being stone dead. It is not the bread and water I fear: I can live on bread: when have I asked for more? It is no hardship to drink water if the water be clean. Bread has no sorrow

Chapter Six

for me, and water no affliction. But to shut me from the light of the sky and the sight of the fields and flowers; to chain my feet so that I can never again ride with the soldiers nor climb the hills; to make me breathe foul damp darkness, and keep from me everything that brings me back to the love of God when your wickedness and foolishness tempt me to hate Him: all this is worse than the furnace in the Bible that was heated seven times.

(Scene 6)

The temptation for the actor playing Joan is great. A young girl is facing the unimaginable throes of horrific capital punishment, at the very edge of agony, welling anger, shame, fear, and dishonor; she looks within herself to discover spiritual power and a sense of rising righteousness. The temptation to *behaviorize* one's performance, to unleash flights of wild emotion, is certainly great—and understandable. After all, actors want to "act" and this passage seems to scream for some all-out acting. But a closer look at the text might reveal another way to interpret—and deliver—this speech. Look at the precise orchestration of Joan's *language*. She uses figures of balance, with a distinct preference for extended antithesis:

Things Joan *can* tolerate	vs.	**Things Joan *cannot* tolerate**
Bread and Water ("I can live on bread… It is no hardship to drink water…")		Being shut from the light of the sky, the sight of fields and flowers; unable to ride with the soldiers nor climb the hills

Joan sets up a strong tension between what is acceptable and what is not acceptable. She stretches language and she enlivens her message with very clear, vivid differences. You can malnourish my body, she implies, but you cannot malnourish my soul. Additionally, she uses enargia (verbal cinema) to paint graphic images of freedom and natural beauty. For both antithesis and enargia, the actor needs to have her wits. She must remain in artistic control of the speech. Yes, Joan has an *action* to play, but she needs to vividly evoke the parade of stunning images and balanced clarity of antithesis to best convey this action. This does not mean that she is immune to emotion, but rather—as theater artist Jewel Walker has observed—that *she is using emotion to serve the language, rather than language to serve emotion.*

That's the key point. Many performers unwittingly undermine the power of this speech by relying almost exclusively on a cascade of gut-wrenching feelings, which inevitably tear at the fabric of the composed text. As a result, audiences cannot follow Joan's argument, cannot see her images, and cannot respond to her simple yet eloquent vision. The speech is too broken up by volleys of spontaneous emoting. The feelings are overpowering the coherency of the verbal craft. Imagine a concert violinist suddenly breaking down in the middle of a Beethoven symphony, emotionally caught up in the tumult and fury of a particular passage, unable to play the notes as written. We might feel sympathy for the violinist but we would also feel considerable disappointment. We would no longer be listening to Beethoven's story.

Ironically, the language itself carries much of Joan's action and her "emotion." If the actor trusts in the words, trusts in Shaw's composition, the power of the speech is magnified tenfold. This awareness and trust is difficult to accept, especially for young performers who want to prove their worth and talent. (And worth and talent are often defined, in the contemporary theater, by torrents of impressive emotion.) To put one's trust in something bigger than oneself—namely, the text—takes time, training, and courage.

Joan continues with her speech:

> I could do without my warhorse; I could drag about in a skirt; I could let the banners and the trumpets and the knights and soldiers pass me and leave me behind as they leave the other women, if only I could still hear the wind in the trees, the larks in the sunshine, the young lambs crying through the healthy frost, and the blessed blessed church bells that send my angel voices floating to me on the wind. But without these things I cannot live; and by your wanting to take them away from me, or from any human creature, I know that your counsel is of the devil, and that mine is of God.

Again, the same verbal strategy. Joan unleashes another round of extended antithesis, featuring the same tension: Things Tolerable versus Things Intolerable. Locked up in the dark dungeon of the Tower, she could accept the

Chapter Six

loss of her warhorse, the absence of the soldiers and banners and trumpets, and she could accept the indignity of wearing a skirt. However, she cannot accept the absence of "the wind in the trees, the larks in the sunshine, the young lambs crying through the healthy frost, and the blessed blessed church bells that send my angel voices floating to me on the wind." Therefore, she implies, she would choose death rather than a life deprived of such experiences. She tops off her defiant speech with a resounding single-line antithesis: "I know that your counsel is of the devil, and that mine is of God."

Look at the graphic wonder of Joan's images. They are lit up in Technicolor tones, presented to us one vivid frame at a time. Such imagery requires an element of *control*. Delivering each image clearly to an audience evokes tremendous emotion—in the listener! The actor may experience a little less so that the audience might experience a little more. The fully charged language allows the audience to *participate* in the ideas, moods, images, feelings. These images and emotions are not simply "experienced" for them by the actor. Indeed, the actor and the audience are partners in creating the play. If the actor's feelings are so predominant, they compromise the verbal craft, and we, the audience, lose a valuable opportunity to hear and experience Shaw's Joan. Put another way, Joan has an action to play. She seeks to justify her decision and fortify her righteousness by graphically illustrating her case, line by line. Joan does not seek the judges' approval; instead, she pleads for her own consent and acceptance. *She needs Shaw's soaring language in order to play this action.*

Verbal Power

Fully charged language is bigger than all of us. We must reach for it. In reaching upwards, we are extended, enlarged, as we gain a new awareness of ourselves. The act of speaking is a continual process of self-discovery. You don't really know who you are until you stand in front of a public forum and speak. Any public forum, be it the Town Hall meeting, a neighborhood gathering, a political rally, a Church convocation, a professional conference, on stage at the Globe Theatre, or before the U.S. Supreme Court. You must stand and deliver a persuasive message; you must fill the forum with your words and your passionate persona. You are no longer the same person introspectively brooding in your private study. You are out in the world, shaping it with your potent words. This act of speaking puts you on a grand adventure toward realizing your self. This is certainly one of the great secrets of classical antiquity.

Earlier centuries knew that the act of speaking—persuasively—held the key to developing the self. We can now begin to understand why Shakespeare's age, for instance, spent an inordinate amount of time stressing verbal style and oratory. Mastery of words allowed a flexible and dramatic self, one that could don various styles, masks, points of view, or perspectives. Public speaking was a daily ritual, in the classroom and in the streets, and it served as a kind of barometer of one's efficacy or success. In the public marketplace, our words are subject to cross-examination, applause and catcalls, counter-statement, further refinement. We receive immediate feedback from an audience and we adjust our performance accordingly. Speaker and listener, listener and speaker, create an exciting dynamic, one that stood at the center of education for centuries.

In today's schoolrooms, how often are young people asked to speak at length? Or to take an oral exam? How many are asked to regularly deliver a well-crafted speech on a particular subject? How many are asked to regularly (or ever?) perform or recite a speech, from history or literature? How many students spend their entire educational careers silently sulking in the back of the room?—their voices never released, their very potential never actualized, an invaluable opportunity for personal growth lost.

This educational context has a direct effect on the training of today's actors. Having been reared in a learning environment that has rarely asked them to develop verbal awareness and craft, they are intimidated by texts that feature verbal pop and spark. They are unsure how to proceed. They fear the potential power of their own voice and the dramatic use of vocal expression. Such things may be unreal or melodramatic, certainly not in keeping with the ultracool vocally monotonous persona projected in many contemporary TV shows and films. In young actors' memories, words have never been exalted, have never been the exhilarating energy-producing catalysts that previous centuries knew them to be. These actors may not know that a rousing, well-orchestrated, courageous speech has the potential to change lives, stir a nation, or alter the course of action. Perhaps no one has told them that for verbally daring plays, "yes, it *is* about the words."

Chapter Six

We have been on an adventure together. Maybe the adventure has featured flashes of revolutionary zeal. Hopefully, the ride has been fun, perhaps even wild at times, and has given you some maps and tools with which to continue the journey. Perhaps the verbal landscape seems a bit more exciting, aglow, and navigable than when you first buckled your seatbelt. Our hope is that you feel confident to continue your own exploration, seeing words as a vigorous ally, a lightning rod for theatrical expression. Along the way, remember to be patient and kind to yourself. Much of this material is absorbed and mastered gradually, through rigorous practice and time. Remember, too, that humor is a wonderful antidote to frustration. Take that speech-on-paper, fold it into an aerodynamic shape, and let it fly. It may also remind you that words delight in flying high, spinning around, gliding lightly and whimsically, free of tension.

Persuasive rhetorical language is the flame, a light, continually fanned by our bravest, most passionate impulses. Today let us seek to bring this burning light into the theater. Its primary courier is the actor. This light requires an incendiary actor, one who produces spark and a charismatic charge by extraordinary insistence on the word and its magical resources. He does not rely on manmade technology to create power, but on the voice and its tremendous resources of expression. She puts her faith in the enchanting spirit of storytelling. The persuasive actor today stands in tribute to many predecessors, who have carried the torch over the mountains and through the valleys, across the millennia. Sometimes the flame dimmed, staggered, and was almost extinguished; at other times it flickered back to life.

Now it is in your hands.

Glossary

Accumulatio: A "heaping up." A steamrolling barrage of descriptive words or phrases that generates persuasive power. Verbal crescendo. A figure of amplification.

Amplificatio: "Enlargement," which describes a major rhetorical category—Amplification.

Antithesis: Call and response. One word or phrase plays off another word or phrase. Vocal stretch between two points. A figure of balance.

Appositio: A Latin term related to the placing of something "side by side." The renaming of a person or thing. The various juxtaposed nouns sit "side by side" with the subject. See *Epexegesis*. A figure of amplification.

Asyndeton: The deliberate omission of conjunctions between words or phrases, giving the language a kind of sparse, skeletal, staccato energy. Opposite of *polysyndeton*.

Auxesis: The use of an extraordinary or heightened word in place of an ordinary, habitual word. A figure of amplification.

Commoratio: Repetition of an *idea* in different words. Speaker stresses a main point by repeating it in different words, sharpening it several times for razor-like emphasis. A figure of repetition (ideas).

Deliberatio: A deliberation. The character weighs or "deliberates" various courses of action, pits one outcome against another. A technique of argument and a figure of balance.

Diazeugma: One subject feeds many verbs, creating a heightened sequence of action. A figure of amplification.

Enargia: Cinema of words. A speaker's ability to evoke visually powerful description and to portray it with such graphic immediacy that the listener feels that he, in effect, is seeing the described event "before his eyes." A figure of description.

Glossary

Epexegesis: An "explanation." Refinement of a thought or a renaming of a person or thing. See *Appositio*. A heightening process. A figure of amplification.

Epimone: Cyclical repetition of a phrase in order to emphasize a particular point; the phrase arrives after an interval, like a refrain in music. A figure of repetition (words).

Epizeuxis: An obsessive mantra, this device gathers emphatic power by continually repeating a word or phrase. *Palilogia* on overdrive. A figure of repetition (words).

Exergasia: "Working out." A wide variety of images and viewpoints illumine a single idea or thought. A more complex version of *commoratio*. A figure of repetition (ideas).

Homeric Simile: An epic comparison of two things, utilizing a setup-payoff structure. This AS/SO structure is preceded by a specific *action* that draws the simile into play.

Homoieteleuton: Same word endings. Derives its power from the seductive chemistry created when word endings continually collide in similar sounds, as in many Hip-Hop lyrics. A figure of repetition (sound).

Hypophora: Q&A strategy. The speaker poses a question and then immediately answers it, using a distinct "persona" for each. Two voices. A figure of balance.

Isocolon: Rhythmic swing. A series of clauses, of similar length and same grammatical structure, are strung together to create an infectious groove. A figure of repetition (structure).

Metaphor: Transference. Finds a connection between two things, often dissimilar, and compares them. The connection is direct and "taken for granted," as the attributes of one thing are *transferred* to another thing.

Onomatopoeia: Making words. Words are echoing or imitating natural sounds. "The tea kettle *hissed* its fury." A subset of *Enargia*, a figure of description.

Palilogia: The immediate repetition of a phrase or word, back-to-back. A blast of vehemence. Recapitulation. A figure of repetition.

Polysyndeton: The deliberate use of conjunctions between words or phrases, giving the language a rhythmic, sweeping energy. Opposite of *asyndeton*.

Glossary

Punchline Simile: A riddle-like comparison that, after the listener's interest is aroused, is followed with an explanatory punchline. (author term)

Rhetoric: The art of persuasion by words. Focuses on the power of words to influence a situation, particularly in public assemblies. Beginning in the 5th century B.C. in the West, protocols were initiated to describe the elements of effective speaking and how these elements could be taught to young students.

Showoff Simile: A fun, outrageous form of simile, often used for witty, deliberately self-conscious display. (author term)

Simile: Latin term for "like." Explicitly compares two elements not normally associated with one another, building an overt bridge between them by using "like" or "as" in the comparison. Therefore, an *explicit* form of metaphor.

Verbal Tango: Two characters "dance together," sharing metaphorical code words in a scene. One character introduces a "step," which is picked up and expanded by the partner with a "counter-step," developing a witty verbal exchange or *transference*. (author term)

Suggestions for Further Reading

Joseph, Sister Miriam. *Shakespeare's Use of the Arts of Language*. Philadelphia, 2008, reprint.

>This pioneering work is a comprehensive analysis of the rhetorical devices Shakespeare utilized in his plays. Presented against a backdrop of the intensive Elizabethan grammar school training that Shakespeare was almost certain to have received.

Kennedy, George A. *A New History of Classical Rhetoric*. Princeton, 1994.

>This is "the Bible." A foundational work that traces the origins and development of the art of rhetoric, from the early Greeks, to the Romans, to the Middle Ages.

Lanham, Richard A. *A Handlist of Rhetorical Terms, Second Edition*. Berkeley, Los Angeles, and London, 1991.

>An A–Z dictionary of the hundreds of rhetorical devices, patterns, and figures that have accumulated from the ancient Greeks to the present day. A beginner's guide, an introduction into the world of verbal persuasion, and, as such, a great resource for performers.

Nash, Walter. *Rhetoric: The Wit of Persuasion*. Oxford, 1992, reprint.

>Buoyant and insightful, this book explores the myriad ways crafted language recruits us, moves us, persuades us, gives us pleasure, makes us complicit, from the wit of advertising slogans to the carefully designed words of an Emily Dickenson poem.

Credits and Acknowledgments

The author and publisher wish to thank the following, who have given permission for the use of copyright material:

Red © John Logan, 2009 by kind permission of Oberon Books Ltd.

Hedda © 2008 Lucy Kirkwood, by kind permission of Nick Hern Books, London, http://www.nickhernbooks.co.uk.

Excerpts from *Travesties*, copyright © 1975 by Tom Stoppard. Used by permission of Grove/Atlantic, Inc. Any third-party use of this material, outside of this publication, is prohibited.

Travesties, by Tom Stoppard; published by Faber and Faber, Ltd.

From *Iliad*, translated by Stanley Lombardo (Copyright © 1997, Hackett Publishing Co.). Reprinted by permission of the publisher.

© 1998, Sarah Kane, pub. 1998, *Crave*, published by Methuen Drama, an imprint of Bloomsbury Publishing Plc. 2006 Estate of Sarah Kane.

© 1989, Jim Cartwright, pub. 1989, *Road*, published by Methuen Drama, an imprint of Bloomsbury Publishing Plc.

Quadrille © NC Aventales AG, 1952, by permission of Alan Brodie Representation Ltd., http://www.alanbrodie.com.

Excerpt(s) from *The Iliad* by Homer, translated by Robert Fagles, translation copyright © 1990 by Robert Fagles. Used by permission of Viking Books, an imprint of Penguin Publishing Group, a division of Penguin Random House LLC. All rights reserved.

Credits and Acknowledgments

MLK excerpts: Reprinted by arrangement with The Heirs to the Estate of Martin Luther King Jr., c/o Writers House as agent for the proprietor New York, NY. Copyright: © 1963 Dr. Martin Luther King, Jr. © renewed 1991 Coretta Scott King.

Topdog/Underdog by Suzan-Lori Parks. Copyright © 1999, 2001, 2002 by Suzan-Lori Parks. Published by Theatre Communications Group. Used by permission of Theatre Communications Group.

Slavs! by Tony Kushner. Published in *Thinking About the Longstanding Problems of Virtue and Happiness*. Copyright © 1995 by Tony Kushner. Published by Theatre Communications Group. Used by permission of Theatre Communications Group.

Homebody/Kabul by Tony Kushner. Copyright © 2000, 2001, 2002, 2004 by Tony Kushner. Published by Theatre Communications Group. Used by permission of Theatre Communications Group.

A Murder of Crows. Copyright © 2006 by Mac Wellman. All rights reserved. Reprinted by Playscripts, Inc. To purchase acting editions of this play, or to obtain stock and amateur performance rights, you must contact: Playscripts, Inc.
website: http://www.playscripts.com
phone: 1-866-NEW-PLAY (639-7529)

Quake. Copyright © 2005 by Melanie Marnich. All rights reserved. Reprinted by Playscripts, Inc. To purchase acting editions of this play, or to obtain stock and amateur performance rights, you must contact: Playscripts, Inc.
website: http://www.playscripts.com
phone: 1-866-NEW-PLAY (639-7529)

Language of Angels. Copyright © 2002 by Naomi Iizuka. All rights reserved. Reprinted by Playscripts, Inc. To purchase acting editions of this play, or to obtain stock and amateur performance rights, you must contact: Playscripts, Inc.
website: http://www.playscripts.com
phone: 1-866-NEW-PLAY (639-7529)

The Search for Cindy. Copyright © 2005 by Tim Kochendurfer. All rights reserved. Reprinted by Playscripts, Inc. To purchase acting editions of this

Credits and Acknowledgments

play, or to obtain stock and amateur performance rights, you must contact: Playscripts, Inc.
website: http://www.playscripts.com
phone: 1-866-NEW-PLAY (639-7529)

Excerpts from *Big Love* and *bobrauschenbergamerica*, by kind permission of Charles Mee, playwright.

Excerpts from *On the Verge* and *In a Pig's Valise*, by kind permission of Eric Overmyer, playwright.

Excerpt from *Bad Penny*, by kind permission of Mac Wellman, playwright.

Excerpt from *Lift and Bang*, by kind permission of Julie Marie Myatt, playwright.

Excerpts from *The Evidence of Silence Broken: A Spoken-Word Performance Concert*, by kind permission of Zell Miller III, poet/playwright.

Excerpt from *The Dance*, by kind permission of Kim Euell, playwright.

Art Credit:

Original illustrations by artist Arielle Jessop (http://www.ariellejessop.com).

Publication Subvention Grant:

University of Massachusetts Amherst

Index

accent: in amplificatory figures, 56, 58; in balanced figures, 4, 5, 19; in metaphor, 98; in repetition, 142; in verbal tango, 106. See also stress
accumulatio: definition of, 28; in long-distance, 34–38; in overview, 39; in renaming, 41; in short track, 28–32; in two characters, 33–34; with antithesis, 158–159. See also verbal drive
action: in contemporary actor training, xiii, 131; in amplification, 41–42, 57–58; in Homeric simile, 111–112, 114; in image and description, 61, 67, 79, 92; in language-driven performance, 162, 164; in metaphor, 99
actor training: in contemporary America, xi, xviii–xix, 6; in cultural landscape, 59
Aeschylus, xvii; *The Suppliant Women*, 10
amplificatio, 27
amplification: origins of, 27; strategy of, xviii; overview of, 58–59
antithesis: definition of, 2; in cascading stretch, 10–11; in deliberatio, 23, 25; in double stretch, 6–9; in outrageous uses, 12–13; in repetition,127; in stretching text, 1, 3–6, 8, 13, 162–164; in tandem with amplification, 158–159
apate, 95
appositio: 28, 39, 41, 59; definition of, 40; obsessive renaming in, 43, 45; overview of, 46
Aristotle, xvii, 62; on metaphor, 95, 99, 101; *Rhetoric*, 95
AS/SO structure, in Homeric simile, 111–113, 116. See also LIKE/SO structure

asyndeton, 58
auxesis: definition of, 37; in character insight, 49, 52–52; in four amplificatory figures, 28; in overview, 59; in playful world, 46

balance, strategy of, viii, xviii, 1, 5, 9, 21, 26, 162
Barton, John, 2
behavioral dialogue, xiii
big band jazz, 57, 150, 153
"call and response": in antithesis 2, 8; in Homeric simile, 115, 117
Cartwright, Jim, *Road*, 137
Chandler, Raymond, 50, 120
characterismus, 61
charged language, xviii, 164. See also heightened language
commoratio, 142–145, 147; definition of, 141
Congreve, William, *The Way of the World*, 22–23, 55–56, 154
Cooper, Lane, 95
correspondences, 110, 112, 115–117
Coward, Noel, *Quadrille*, 82
crescendo, 29, 32, 34, 42, 133, 137, 157

Davis, Bette, 59
deliberatio, 1, 22–23; definition of, 21; stunning uses in, 25
Demosthenes, xvii
description, in enargia, xviii; 60–63, 68, 77, 80, 92. See also image
detective lingo, 51, 120
detonation (vocal), 9, 53, 58
diazeugma, 28, 54, 57, 59; definition of, 55

downglides/down-endings (vocal), 32–33, 41, 57
Dryden, John, *Marriage à la Mode*, 118

editing (vocal): in contemporary plays, 81, 83, 89; in *Iliad*, 68–70; in overview, 92; in Shakespeare, 71, 75, 77
electronica, electronic media, 60, 92
enargia: definition of, 62; in classical training, 61–63; in contemporary plays, 79–80, 82, 90–91, 99; in filmmaking, 64, 68, 75–76, 92; in *Iliad*, 63, 92; in *Saint Joan*, 162; in Shakespeare, 70–71, 76, 92; in verbal ownership, 66–67, 90. *See also* verbal cinema
energounta, 95
epexegesis, 39
epimone, 127, 129–131, 133–135, 139–141; definition of, 126
epizeuxis, 137–141; definition of, 136
Euell, Kim, *The Dance*, 153
exergasia, 147; definition of, 145
explanation, in appositio, 39–40, 43

fables, in metaphor, 98–99, 101–102, 115,
Fagles, Robert, 111
filmmaking terms, in enargia, 64, 68–70, 72–75, 92

geographia, 61
Globe Theatre, 40, 70, 78, 113
Goodman, Benny, 150, 153
Grant, Cary, 59

heightened text, xviii, xx. *See also* charged language
Hip-Hop, rhythm of, xv, 153–155
Hip-Hop Theater, xvi, xix
Homer, 63, 111
Homeric simile, 110–111, 113, 117, 122
homoioteleuton, definition of, 153–154; 153, 155. *See also* Hip-Hop
hydrographia, 61

hypophora: definition of, 14; in classical training, 21; in contemporary Q&A, 19–20; in deliberatio, 23; in rhetorical balance, 1; in two voices, 15–18

I have a dream, 124–125, 128, 157
Ibsen, Henrik, *Hedda Gabler*, 90
Iizuka, Naomi, *Language of Angels*, 81
Iliad, The, xix; amplification in, 40; enargia in, 67, 92; history of, 63; Homeric simile in, 111
image: in enargia, 60–62, 64, 67–69, 71, 76–77, 79, 82, 90–92; in metaphor, 99; in *Richard III*, 146–147; in *Saint Joan*, 162–164. *See also* description
incantation, 126
inflection: in amplification, 57; in phrasing, 35–37; in speaking, 4, 7, 9, 13, 15, 19, 26; in verbal tango, 106, 108. *See also* pitch
insistence, in speaking, 41–42, 44, 46, 156
intention, in actor training, 9, 102, 108, 112, 147, 161
invisible language, xii–xiii
isocolon, 148, 151–153; definition of, 149. *See also* rhythmic swing
Isocrates, xvii

Jackson, Peter, 25

Kane, Sarah, *Crave*, 37
Kennedy, George, xvii
Kennedy, John F., 125
King, Jr., Dr. Martin Luther, 2, 124–125, 128, 157
Kirkwood, Lucy, *Hedda*, 90
Kochendurfer, Tim, *The Search for Cindy*, 138
Kushner, Tony, xvi, 137; *Homebody/Kabul*, 49; *Slavs!*, 54, 136, 158

language-driven actor training, xix, 54, 59, 138, 141, 159–160
language plays, xvi
Lanham, Richard, xviii, 62

175

Index

level glides (vocal), 33
LIKE/SO structure, in Homeric simile, 114–115. *See also* AS/SO
liveliness and surprise, in metaphor, 95–96, 99–100, 102
Logan, John, *Red*, 20
Lombardo, Stanley, 64, 68
Lysias, xvii, 62

magic carpet, 94, 96, 99, 103, 109, 123
Marnich, Melanie, *Quake*, 30, 33–34, 151
mantras, xviii, 136–139, 141, 155
Marston, John, *The Malcontent*, 30–31, 149
Mee, Charles, *Big Love*, 10–11; *bobrauschenbergamerica*, 141, 143
metaphor: definition of, 95; in punchline simile, 119; in Shakespeare, 96–97, 99, 101, 103; in Wilde, 103–104; strategy of, xviii
metaphorical run, 96–98, 101, 103, 106, 122–123; playing in same key, 104–109. *See also* verbal tango
Miller III, Zell, *The Evidence of Silence Broken*, xv, xvi, 139
Milton, John, 14, 129; *Paradise Lost*, 14–15, 129
Myatt, Julie Marie, *Lift and Bang*, xii

naturalism, 6, 20, 50, 120, 150, 155

Odyssey, The, 67, 111
onomatopoeia, 62, 75; definition of, 76
orators, early Greek "rock stars," xvii
Overmyer, Eric, *In a Pig's Valise*, 42, 50, 110, 120–122; *On the Verge*, 79
Ovid, *Metamorphosis*, 70
owning the image, 66–67, 71, 80

palilogia, 133, 135–137, 139–141; definition of, 134
Parks, Suzan-Lori, xvi, 134; *Topdog/Underdog*, 132, 134, 148, 159
passion to communicate, 4, 9, 19, 26, 37, 160

Persuasion, persuasive power: xi, xvii–xix, 3, 6, 14, 16, 19, 26–28, 30, 34, 37, 102–103, 126–128, 143, 147–148, 154–155, 157–158, 160, 164–165
phrasing, 35–36, 41–42, 44, 46, 119, 150–151
pitch, in speaking, 4, 9, 32, 105, 112, 128. *See also* inflection
polysyndeton, 38
pragmatographia: definition of, 61; in *Iliad*, 67–68
protagonist and antagonist, in hypophora, 17–19
punchline simile, 117–119. *See also* setup and punchline structure
Puritan Commonwealth, 109

"realistic" pauses, 29. *See also* "searching" moments
renaming, 40–44, 46, 58. *See also* appositio
repetition: in epimone, 126–128, 133; in epizeuxis, 136–138; in ideas, 141–145; in palilogia, 133–136; in sound, 153, 155–156; in structure and rhythm, 147–152; in tandem, 140–141; strategy of, xviii, 125, 139
Restoration Theater, xvi, 22, 55, 104, 108–109, 118, 131, 154
Rhetoric: art of, xix–xx; birth of, xvi–xvii; definition of, xvii; training in, xvi, 47, 61, 67, 126, 157
rhetorike, definition of, xvii
rhetorical devices, xvii–xviii, 158. *See also* rhetorical figures
rhetorical figures, xvii–xviii; definition of, xviii, 1; 126, 129, 138, 158–160. *See also* rhetorical devices
rhythm: in amplificatory figures, 32; in balanced figures, 4–5, 9, 13, 19, 26; in metaphorical language, 102, 112; in repetition, 132, 147–149, 152–154; in verbal tango, 108
rhythmic swing, 38, 149–151, 160. *See also* isocolon
Richards, I. A., 95

Index

"searching" moments, 29, 142, 150.
   See also "realistic" pauses
Serkis, Andy, 25
setup and payoff structure: in Homeric simile, 110–114, 116, 119; in hypophora, 16–17, 20
setup and punchline structure, 117–119.
   See also punchline simile
Shakespeare, William
   —general: in company actors, xx; in dramatic characters, 5, 22, 48, 159; in enargia, 61, 70, 75–76, 78, 92; in Globe, 40, 70, 113; in grammar school training, xvii, 21, 48, 70, 165; in simile structure, 117
   —works: *As You Like It*, 22; *Henry IV, Pt.1*, 16–17; *Henry V*, 70–71; *Henry VI, Pt. 2*, 100, 103; *Henry VI, Pt. 3*, 40–41, 113; *King John*, 96; *Love's Labour's Lost*, 47–48; *Macbeth*, 3, 44–45; *Midsummer Night's Dream*, 81; *Othello*, 130–131, 135–136; *Richard II*, 45; *Richard III*, 17–19, 145; *Two Gentlemen of Verona*, 116
Shaw, George Bernard, 6, 19, 159; *Getting Married*, 127; *Major Barbara*, 6–8; *Man and Superman* "Don Juan in Hell" interlude, 12–13; *Mrs. Warren's Profession*, 19–20; *The Philanderer*, 141; *Saint Joan*, 161–164
showoff simile, 120
simile, definition of, 110; 111–117 passim, 121
slang, 51
Sophocles, xvii
sound and rhythm, xi, xv, 58, 127, 139, 154, 156, 160
source and vehicle: in metaphor, 95, 97, 99; in simile, 110, 114–117
spells and grooves, 140, 148, 154–155
Spoken Word, xix, 139
Stoppard, Tom, xvi; *Travesties*, xiii–xvi, 8–9, 28–29, 138, 154, 159
storyboard, 71, 83
stress: in amplificatory figures, 32, 56–57; in balanced figures, 4, 5, 7, 9, 13, 26; in image, 69; in metaphorical language, 98, 102; in repetition of sound, 154; in simile, 112; in verbal tango, 105, 108. See also accent
subtext, xii–xiii, xv, xviii–xix, 102, 108, 159, 161
surface text, xv–xvi, 102, 108–109. See also verbal surface

This is like That, 113, 115, 117, 122–123. See also simile
Tolkien, J. R. R., *Lord of the Rings/The Two Towers*, 25
tone (vocal), 69, 89, 102
transference, 95–98, 100, 102–104, 109, 119, 122
"turnarounds," 23–24

upglides (vocal), 33

Vanbrugh, John, *The Relapse*, 23, 104
verbal cinema, 157, 159, 162. See also enargia
verbal drive: in amplification, 28–29, 32–33, 35–36, 39, 41, 159; in repetition, 141. See also accumulatio
verbal surface, xii, xv, xvii–xviii, 102, 108–109, 159. See also surface text
verbal tango, 104–109, 122. See also metaphorical run
Vico, Giambattista, 98
Virgil, *Aeneid*, 70
visible language, xv, 159
volume: in speaking, 4–5, 9, 13, 19, 26, 32

Walker, Jewel, 163
Wellman, Mac, 34; *Bad Penny*, 31, 34–35; *A Murder of Crows*, 43–44
Wilde, Oscar, 143; *The Importance of Being Earnest*, xiii; *An Ideal Husband*, 103–104
Wilson, August, xvi
Wycherley, William, *The Country Wife*, 118

zeugma, 55